Hungry for Life

FINDING PERMANENT
FREEDOM FROM FOOD GUILT

MARLA JONES

ARK
house

Ark House Press
PO Box 1722, Port Orchard, WA 98366 USA
PO Box 1321, Mona Vale NSW 1660 Australia
PO Box 318 334, West Harbour, Auckland 0661 New Zealand
arkhousepress.com

Cataloguing in Publication Data:
Title: Hungry For Life
ISBN: 978-0-6487607-8-8 (pbk.)
Subjects: Christian Living; Biography;
Other Authors/Contributors: Jones, Marla

Design and layout by initiateagency.com

thank you

This book is dedicated to the many beautiful women I have met on this journey, a couple of very brave men and to you. If you have picked up this book for yourself, I want you to know that I understand. I am praying for you; that God will speak life through this book and into your heart. I pray for freedom from any eating issues you may have.

If you have picked this book up to understand someone going through eating issues, thank you. Thank you for caring.

I cannot speak enough of my God who has always been an ever source of help in my times of trouble. Thank you God for allowing me to be a part of your work in changing people's lives. It has been an honor to see you at work; healing, installing hope and setting people free.

I would like to thank my husband for being a part of my healing and always seeing the diamond that lay deep within. I will forever love you.

Thank you to Jamie, Eric and Tracy for getting this off the ground; my spiritual warriors Carole, Glenyse and Tracy and the rest of my BOL team Joanne, Kate, Tiffany. Thank you for supporting me. Thank you Diana for your beautiful cover artwork.

Finally thank you to all the leaders of the course 'Bite of Life' who have shared their lives so others may be healed. May the truth be known and continue to set people free.

Table of Contents

Introduction

God is strong, and he wants you strong. So take everything the Master has set out for you, well-made weapons of the best materials. And put them to use so you will be able to stand up to everything the devil throws your way. This is no afternoon athletic contest that we'll walk away from and forget about in a couple of hours. This is for keeps, a life-or-death fight to the finish against the devil and all his angels. Be prepared.

Ephesians 6:12 (The Message)

The aim of this book is to prepare you for the battles; the spiritual battles that lay behind the physical battles. And yes, this book is designed for battles around the issues of food but the principles taught here will help you battle anything that holds you captive. God is all about freedom. He sent His Son to die for your freedom. God holds the spiritual tools that you need to acquire that freedom.

I can not emphasize enough that our Lord is interested in every aspect of your life. You can not segment your life into spiritual and non spiritual areas. Every area is of spiritual concern to God. He loves you so much. God is not limited to a church building on Sundays and is not restricted to certain times or experiences in your life.

'For our struggle is not against flesh and blood, but against rulers, against the authorities and against the spiritual forces of evil in the heavenly realms.'
Ephesians 6:12 (NIV)

He is an 'all-in' God. He makes it clear that he does not like the fence sitters who only want to dip their toes in the sea of God's immeasurable power and glory. He wants all of you and wants to help you in every area of your life.

My aim is to show that your eating is of spiritual concern to God and that He has the answers you need if you have struggled with any area of food or self image problems. Even if you are not a Christian or haven't heard much about God, I want to encourage you that God loves you and knows everything about you. He loves you regardless of how you feel about Him and no matter what you have done in your life, nothing can stop God from giving you a fresh start. He is the God of second chances and only waits for your invitation.

God loves us and wants us to be free but He will not compromise His holiness to do it 'our way'. It has to be us who change. We have to come to Him. The biggest thing standing in our way most of the time is our own attitude. It is not easy to admit you have a problem nor is it easy to utterly depend on someone else for the way out of that problem. But this is the key to finding freedom forever.

Once a very wounded soldier myself in the battle of food addiction, I understand what it is like to have tried 'everything' and end up at a seemingly endless dark pit wondering, 'Where is God?' I studied every nutrition book to the last letter, knew the nutritional information of every food that ever existed, tried every diet in the Western World I could find, worked in the fitness industry and did endless hours of sport and exercise and yet never found the answers I needed to get out of the endless cycle of dieting, food addictions, poor self image and hopelessness.

Although I was a young Christian through out most of my struggles, I simply did not have the revelation of God's freedom that I needed to be set free forever. I didn't think that God cared about my struggle in this area of my life and that it was up to me to find the answers.

I, like many other Christians, looked to the world to solve what Jesus himself wanted to teach me.

It concerns me that there are more diet centers on every corner dealing with this problem then churches.

When I turned to the church for help I found that not many understood what I was going through and offered well intended advice that actually made things worse. I knew some kind souls really cared about me but were at a loss as to what to say or do to help me. Other people were very judgmental and quite harsh with their words. This is what I want to change. When people come into the church for help, I want us to be ready!

Please understand that I am not against the nutritional and health advice of the systems of this world. It's just they only hold a very small portion of the answers one needs to walk free of this forever. If the world held all of the answers then why is the dieting industry growing and growing? If diets worked, why do people keep going back to them? If it worked you should never have to return to another diet ever again. If you are healed you won't even think about this area of your life with worry or discontent.

It concerns me that there are more diet centers on every corner dealing with this problem then churches. That Christian people feel they have to find someplace outside of the church to help them. Not only do I want Christians to realize that God holds all of the answers they are looking for but that He wants to train and use the church body to help others.

I write this book as one who has been healed. For over twenty years I have lived life in the way God has designed; with joy and freedom! It saddens me when I see others still trapped in the system I used to be trapped in. I want every person to experience this joy, the way life is intended to be lived. My prayer is for you is this: If you are trapped in a life you do not want to lead anymore, may you find freedom. If you are reading this book in order to understand and support others who struggle in this area of life, may you find wisdom and compassion to respond in a way that brings healing.

I do not hold all of the answers for you but I know the One who does. May this book lead you closer to Him and may you find comfort in His care for you.

Lord, you have brought light to my life; my God, you light up my darkness. In your strength I can crush an army; with my God I can scale any wall.

As for God, his way is perfect. All the Lord's promises prove true. He is a shield for all who look to him for protection. For who is God except the Lord? Who but our God is a solid rock?

God arms me with strength; he has made my way safe. He makes me as surefooted as a deer, leading me safely along the mountain heights. He prepares me for battle; he strengthens me to draw a bow of bronze. You have given me the shield of your salvation. Your right hand supports me; your gentleness has made me great. You have made a wide path for my feet to keep them from slipping.

Psalm 18:28- 36 (NIV)

Chapter One
Freedom

I am free from an eating disorder that gripped me for at least seven years of my life. It is not easy to classify this 'disorder' as it doesn't neatly fit into any category. Many people believe eating disorders fall into one of two categories: anorexia or bulimia. I believe an eating 'disorder' includes **any** battle involving food. Going from one diet to another, not being able to lose weight and keep it off, avoiding foods because they affect the body in some negative way, not being able to eat due to stress or medical problems, thinking about food all the time or being overly focused on physical appearance, being addicted to physical fitness or fashion regimes. Some people suffer with combined categories of eating disorders; I suffered with just about all of them.

It is hard to even put a time frame on when it began but I can remember clearly the day that it ended. I was completely healed by the hand of God. I had been healed for about ten years and was, quite honestly, happy to have lived my life never giving thought to it again, until God spoke.

If you have never heard the voice of God it is quite hard to understand what it is like. Although I will write more of this later, for now let it suffice for me to say that when He spoke I was awakened in the middle of the night to a vision of many people crying out for help.

God showed me thousands and thousands of people held captive by the very same problem that I have been healed of. He was angry that his children suffered so and spoke the word, 'Enough'. He began to reveal to me the in depth meaning of His word day after day and placed in my heart the desire to set others free. Now I do so with the Lord's grace and power, to help others like me to become free from this bondage.

Before I share my story I want to make sure that we are on the same page in understanding my view of an easting disorder.

My Definition: An eating disorder is something that holds a person captive, the opposite of living in complete freedom in the way God has designed us to live. Characteristics of eating disorders are as varied as the eating disorders themselves. Some common signs of a person struggling in an eating disorder include thinking about and planning the perfect diet and commonly breaking that diet in utter dismay. The person may struggle with depression and anger. There may be lack of meaning to life and loss of hope that things will ever change. Thoughts of how one looks physically may torment the person day and night. Secret eating is common, especially if the food is considered 'fattening'. Shyness and low self-esteem may be evident.

Eating disorders are similar to many other serious addictions in that those involved will mask it, hide it, avoid addressing it because of their firm belief that no one could understand what they are going through. And let us not simplify this addiction. There are just as many side affects to this disease including minor to very serious health problems, mental problems such as depression and unfortunately many deaths.

Yet an eating disorder is so different from other addictions in the sense that this is one addiction you cannot avoid. We have to eat to survive. We can't join a group and commit to avoid food altogether. So we try to go to a group to learn how to control it. Again this is absolutely absurd as it is for a heroin addict to try and control the amount of heroin consumed each day. When you are addicted you are out of control. For many, they can control it for a period of time, sometimes a long period of time and it may even look outwardly like they are fine. But it's the inner thoughts that torment, 'you're not good enough, you'll never be good enough'. Or the person is so focused on a diet regime that they can't talk about anything else, unseemingly able to just let go and enjoy life.

In the case of a drug addiction, if the problem is revealed, others can help by restraining them in such a way until they can get a handle on life and learn how to live life without drugs. People, who struggle with food and physically show this struggle being overweight, hear the comments of others around them. They are made fun of, teased, treated shamefully and abused verbally and sometimes even physically abused. It is no wonder they hesitate to ask for help from a society that has treated them so poorly.

When they do finally muster up the courage to try and ask for help, they are met with pat answers like 'it can't be as bad as you imagine, just stop eating so much', 'just don't eat dessert', 'don't worry about the way you look', 'you look fine to me' and 'I'm sure it will pass' No wonder the eating disorder sufferer remains silent. Many times they are treated as if they are just plain stupid.

They already feel crazy enough without anyone else's help. So they go on this path of life alone, isolated. Everyone else eats food normally, why can't I? How can I be addicted to the very thing I need to survive? Many secretly wish that they would die to escape this torment. They search for answers everywhere to try and fight the battles of their problems but when they fall back into the very same situations, they find themselves empty not knowing where to look anymore for help. The end result is feeling utterly hopeless.

Christians are not immune to eating disorders. In fact, it is mainly in churches that I run most of my seminars. Christians not only suffer with eating disorders but they feel even worse thinking that even God has abandoned them. They are even more afraid to talk about their situation as others might see them as not having enough faith in God. They search the Bible for answers and feel that it does not address the issues of food very much. Many have been coerced into trying 'Biblical diets'. They try eating only fruit and vegetables like Daniel or starving themselves in the name of fasting. They follow what others label under God's name instead of being guided by the creator himself. They place their trust in a man made system instead of putting trust in a Holy God who loves them.

The true test of whether or not you are in the will of God is if you are experiencing the fruits of his spirit; love, joy, peace, patience, kindness, goodness, faithfulness, gentleness and self-control. (Galatians 5:22 NIV) I have not found a person yet who states they experience these while dieting. Have you ever heard someone say, 'I love dieting, it brings me such joy and peace and I find it has developed in me such patience with those around me'.

You may have gathered by now that I am anti-diet. Only in the sense of what a diet means. In my mind I see the word 'diet' as meaning for a period of time a person will only eat what is on a scheduled plan and exercise according to that plan. The problem with most diets is that they are only for a period of time and when the person ends that time, they go back to where they started. When people are on 'diets' they become almost a different person controlled by a system and unable to relate normally to the society of people around them. I am all for educating people on nutritional aspects of food. I feel this should be included more and more into our schools so that children understand how to cook and eat healthy meals.

I am concerned however, that there are more diet centers than churches dealing with such problems. I am saddened by the amount of people in the church struggling with this problem and by all the 'well meaning' comments offered by people of the church who have no understanding of the situation.

It's a shame that people put all of their trust in a person running a diet centre or a diet so freely, yet hesitate to share with the family of the church. Christians need to be trained in the word of God on how to deal with these problems. I hope that through reading this book three things will be accomplished; The reader will be released from a problem that most likely has plagued them for far too long, that the church will become equipped to help the masses in their own congregations and in the community and finally that all of us will begin to understand the love of God and His desire to be part of every aspect of our lives.

If you are not involved in an eating disorder yourself, most likely you are surrounded by people who are.

I want to start by saying to you the reader, that if you struggle from an eating disorder of any kind, I do understand. I will qualify this by sharing with you some of the memories of my past. I share them openly because people who are involved in eating disorders do not. The absolute anguish and agony of being in an eating disorder is the bondage to silence.

If you are not involved in an eating disorder yourself, most likely you are surrounded by people who are. They live life amazingly well, conquering just about everything that comes their way because they are unable to conquer the hidden problem held deep within. Although I have been involved deeply within these disorders, even I can not recognize the problem easily in others without the prompting of the Holy Spirit within me.

I find that it is very helpful now looking back on my own experience as so much is learned from our personal history, hindsight and memories. The difference now is that I look back without pain. I can see all the things that I used to say and do but I no longer feel the emotions behind it. This is what God can do. He can completely eliminate the pain from our memories.

I must start by saying that one could put many reasons to this baggage of struggles, hurt and pain dealt to us in life and usually there are many other people to which one could blame but most of the time I've come to realize my view has been distorted by my own self righteousness. It is hard to recognize that I am at the root cause of most of my problems. But as one popular saying goes; 'Once I am the cause of my problems; I am also potentially the solution.

Notes:

11

Chapter Two
My Story

I t is quite hard to pinpoint when my struggle began. I was always quite self-conscious and was always a 'people pleaser'. I didn't deal with problems very well and tended to store everything inside. I was always too ashamed to admit to anyone I had a problem or struggled with any area of my life so although I was always surrounded by people, I tended to go about life alone.

One of my earliest memories was of a school dance when I was about twelve years old. At that point in my life my Mother strongly influenced what I wore to school each day. I absolutely hated the outfit she wanted me to wear that day to such an 'important' event in my life. Not much really happened that day.

That's all I remember about it, that I had on an outfit that I was so embarrassed about that I stood against the wall the entire time of the dance talking to a girlfriend of mine. I wanted desperately to go out and be a part of the big scene but I froze and couldn't move. Suddenly, I hated everything about the way I looked. I hated my outfit, my big frizzy permed hair, the pimples on my face and the person inside who had no self-confidence.

Sometimes (in fact, I would say most of the time) the most trivial events start major problems in our lives; especially when it comes to addictions. The lure of addictions usually starts in situations that are quite non-threatening yet the pressure of others, whether imagined or real, is very high. Although it doesn't happen over night, the negative thought patterns in the mind begin a slow and subtle change in a person. It is so subtle that it goes unnoticed until it becomes a problem. Little problems compiled up over time without resolution need an outlet and unfortunately the most popular outlet is some form of addiction. Suddenly a person is smack in the middle of a full-blown addiction, wondering where it all started.

Something broke in me that day. It started an outward focus on what other people thought and said about me, so much so that there wasn't much of *me* left. I was too busy trying to act and be what other people wanted, which is why the next four years nearly killed me.

The real struggles began when I entered high school. The pressure placed on how one looked and acted was phenomenal. I was really thrown into deep water and became frantic from the first day. The size of my school probably did not help matters. There were about 2,800 students in my school with more than 730 kids in my class alone! There were so many, that on graduation day I was just introducing myself to the students seated next to me, five minutes before we received our diplomas. With that many people in a school, you had to either be very talented or good looking to be noticed enough to make good friends.

Even the 'talent' that I was involved in placed a lot of emphasis on looks. Ballet was my favorite activity in the world. I loved to dance. Mom enrolled me since I was a little girl to build my confidence and balance. A lot of emphasis was placed on grace and performance.

Then I began my first job at the ice cream parlor. I thought this was the best job in the world because I was able to create ice cream masterpieces. If there were any mistakes, the boss told us to put them in the back freezer and we were welcome to eat them on our breaks, free of charge. We also had discounts for anything we purchased off the menu.

Well, between all the discounts and mistakes, you can imagine that I started to put on some weight. Granted, this didn't happen overnight but a sample here and a topping there did put on the weight a lot quicker than I had expected. This, in itself, didn't really bother me until the comments came.

People that I was really close to, family members and friends, seemed to look at me with a hint of disgust in their eyes or maybe it was embarrassment. I'm not really sure. All I knew was that I had never seen that side of them before and it really hurt. I was mortified by the flippant way they would comment about losing weight. Many suggested that I try starvation diets, fad diets, diets from magazines, exercising to excessive limits and even to try throwing up the food that I had just eaten.

Even my ballet teacher, in front of everyone, said that I would not be able to advance further if I did not lose weight. For the first time, I told my mom I didn't want to take ballet classes any more. This confused my mom, as ballet had always been so important to me. She kept questioning why I would want to give up something I so obviously loved. When I wouldn't give her the reasons why, she finally gave in and stopped taking me to lessons.

I felt so worthless and when mom gave into my request to quit, it was like a confirmation to me that I was a failure. It was the final blow to my self-esteem and I began a cycle of dieting that was to last unbeknownst to me for seven long years.

I remember my first real 'diet'. It was just after I became a Christian and my newly found Christian girlfriends and I came up with this diet concoction: a diet shake for breakfast, an apple for lunch and a bowl of rice for dinner. If we ate any more than that we were to throw it back up. Well, I had only thrown up once in my life previous to that moment and I just knew I couldn't do that. So

14

I did my very best to stay on track but I got so hungry. A few days later I broke down and ate as much as my stomach could hold.

I felt miserable and not only did I feel fat but that I had failed. If my friends could do it why couldn't I? So I went to the cupboard to see if I could erase the problem and continue on like nothing had happened. I found a box of laxatives and thought if I took one it would empty my stomach out. Well, it did and it seemed to work. I got my self-confidence back and didn't tell anyone that I had blown it. Soon all of my self-confidence was based on whether or not I could stick to this diet.

I remember I wanted to sleep everyday when I got home from school because I was so exhausted. My body was still growing and maturing as it was supposed to, yet I was starving it of the nutrition it so desperately needed. But I was losing weight and everyone applauded my effort and gave me such amazing comments. It set in stone my dependence on these comments to how I looked to determine my self-worth.

Well, if you know anything about fad diets, the success is only short term and suddenly you find yourself on the roller coaster of your life. I went from one diet to the next. I tried all the magazine diets, most of the organized, 'civilized' diets and everything and anything in between, spending lots of time and money on each. I started studying every nutrition book I could find. The nutrition books became my other 'Bible', so to speak, as I depended more on what they said than on the real Bible. Although I was a Christian, I thought that God didn't really care about what was happening to me in this area and that the Bible was silent on the issue of dieting.

I entered university with bad habits already formed. Things only became worse. The pressure to study and do well requires a lot of sitting and reading plus lots of food to keep you awake and going. In America, girls normally gain 10 kilos their first year of college because of such changes in lifestyle. Without the critical eyes of friends and family around, I ate what I wanted, when I wanted and let myself get out of control. Suddenly, I found myself at my heaviest weight ever.

I tried everything to get the weight off. I went months at a time eating only vegetables and fruit. Weight shed off easily but as soon as I started eating normally again, it came back at twice the rate! It just didn't make sense. I really can't express how much this absolutely consumed my life. I thought about my weight every minute of the day. I was either planning what I was going to eat or working out how to get rid of what I had already eaten. Amazingly, I kept it all to myself. No one knew how much pain I was in and how much this was affecting me.

Despite what people thought, by this stage I knew everything there was to know about the nutrition side of food and physical training. I could tell you exactly how many calories, grams of fat, carbohydrates and sugar there was in every morsel of food. I had previously coached several others in fitness training. But I just couldn't seem to get control of myself.

I'd start off each day so perfect, eating only what I planned for breakfast and lunch but by four o'clock, my ravished hunger took over and I just gorged myself on food. I would then exercise for two to three hours to work it off, most of the time I would run and run until I threw up. During this time I tried so hard to not take laxatives but after a few days or weeks I would eventually break down and take another laxative.

I felt as if it was the only thing that could completely clean the inside of me out. I felt so awful inside; I would take anything to get rid of that feeling. I became addicted to that feeling of emptiness and what seemed like being back in control again for a short time. I felt so defeated and hopeless.

One time I was so desperate, I finally confided in a close friend of mine. She was overweight but never seemed to be phased by it. She was always so joyful and it seemed she had something I lacked. I would give anything just not to care anymore. So late one night I broke down and told her what I had been doing. It took awhile for her to get over the shock of me using laxatives but then it seemed as though she was suddenly relieved. It was like a light went on and she said, 'what a great idea'. I couldn't believe my ears! Now not only was I hooked, I managed to hook my close friend into my addiction. Apparently, she was very good at hiding her struggle with eating too.

I remember telling my English teacher that I didn't have enough money to cover the English texts we were using in class, yet later in a writing journal I wrote about a new diet book I bought put out by Cher. I was really impressed with it. He was the only person that ever picked up on something seriously going wrong in my life and wrote in my journal confronting me on the fact that if I had enough money to invest in these diet books then I should be able to cover my English texts.

I was so embarrassed that I had been 'caught out' as such. I began to realize the priorities in my life were very messed up from my disorder. It was as if I needed these books to survive while my English texts were optional reading. It is really hard to explain how everything gets so messed up but you are so deceived that you justify all of your actions with excuses that seem like solid reasoning to you.

One of the actions that I am most embarrassed about shows just how trapped I was in this disease. I remember one day blowing my 'diet' again and I went to my room to get some laxatives, but I didn't have any. So when I went to the shop I somehow managed to lose my friends for a few moments to go and grab another box. Well when I looked at the price I realized I hadn't brought enough money. So I hid behind the isle of drugs, opened the box, took one out and put the box back again. It was a fix and nothing would take away my pain until I took that laxative. As you can imagine this was the bottom of the pit for me.

As I was nearing the end of my college experience, I remember one day that completely changed this wretched cycle of dieting madness. During this whole experience, I held onto the hope that God could somehow heal me, if He so desired. I prayed nearly every day for seven years for deliverance from this way of life that seemed to hold me in bondage.

One day I fell to my knees in absolute despair and cried out to God, 'Lord, for seven years I have struggled with this. I have prayed for healing nearly every day of those seven years. Where are you? I can not take any more! I give up! You win! Either heal me of this disease or take my life now. I don't care if I grow to be a two hundred pound woman; I am not going to diet any more!'

A switch clicked. I can't really explain it. It was similar in a way to a light switch in that one minute you are completely lost without hope, in the dark and the next a light comes on and you have this strange new hope, some sort of new life building within you. Now I was not healed in a way that most people imagine. I did not look any different from the outside than I did before that moment but I do believe I was completely and wholly healed from the moment that I truly gave it up to God.

I heard God's voice- not with my ears but with my heart. He was saying to me, 'Now you see as I do; you have no control over your struggles and problems, but I do. By giving it completely to me, I now can help you. I have waited seven years for you to truly trust me to take care of you. Now let me show you how.' I realized that previously, with each prayer, I had given up my problem to God only to take it up again by trying to fix it myself the next day. I didn't trust Him enough to give it completely to him.

Now, that I have the advantage of looking back, I can see quite clearly God's hand upon me each step of the way. He never left me nor did He ever forsake me. The problem obstructed my view of the goodness of God. Knowing this now helps me to trust God whenever I find myself in trouble or in a difficult situation. Although I can't see God at work, He is still there and in control.

Although I was completely healed by God that day, I did not see the physical manifestation of that healing until three and a half years later. The physical weight was actually the last thing to go. As that was not the real problem, as I had previously thought. The real problem was that I did not know who I was or what my purpose was. I had many issues in my life that God needed to address and deal with one by one. When I did finally see the physical results, I did not care any more about weight. I just trusted God to deal with it when He was ready.

This may not sound logical but with God everything is very simple yet nothing is easy.

God had several areas that needed to be addressed in my life and He had a very simple yet personal design for me to follow in order to remain healthy and well. This may not sound logical but with God everything is very simple yet nothing is easy. It was a journey and I had to be open to the many changes God wanted to make in my life. God had specifically declared I was not to take this issue into my own hands ever again. I will never 'diet' again. And I can't express how happy I am to declare that!

At the time of republishing this book, I am celebrating over twenty years of complete freedom in this area of dieting and freedom from a poor self-image. I am content and happy with the way I am. I am free to eat what I want and I am not entrapped in the whole system of vicious cycles. I am focused on what God wants for me and am living with joy in my life.

The main purpose for me telling my story and writing this book is to encourage you to hand your issues over to God and listen to what He has to say to you. I used to think the Bible was silent on the issues of dieting, self-image, women and the issues they face but I am so glad, and relieved, I was wrong. As you will see in this book, God is all but silent. Over several weeks, He continued to guide me and speak to me as I continued to write. This material is just that. I believe God is saying to his people, 'That's enough! It is time for a change!'

In 2 Corinthians 12:9 the Lord says to Paul, 'My grace is sufficient for you, for my power is made perfect in weakness.' Paul then replies, 'Therefore I will boast all the more gladly about my weaknesses, so that Christ's power may rest on me. That is why, for Christ's sake, I delight in weaknesses, in insults, in hardships, in persecutions, in difficulties. For when I am weak, then I am strong.'

Each time I share my story, those who are listening have never ridiculed or laughed or even looked away out of embarrassment; quite the opposite. I see tears of relief from women who realize, maybe for the first time, that they are not alone in their struggles. They see that if I am healed then maybe, just maybe, there is hope for them too.

As I tell my story I continue to learn from it. It allows me to take full responsibility for my own mistakes and shows, in essence, how human I am. All of us have made mistakes, have failed and have fallen short of what we desired to be. The more we come to accept this, the easier it is to get past the shortcomings and get to know each other as the real people we are, the people we want to be and be known for.

It's good to take a long, hard look at your past. We can learn so much from our history. Take the time, no, make the time to specifically write out your story. You could just list the points or if you have a close friend you could talk it over with him or her. Maybe draw your story in different images or symbols.

One way or another, get it out of your head and into the open so that you and God can examine it closely together. This is the best place to begin before you go any further, know where you come from. You don't need to share it with anyone if you don't want to. And after you finish your story you can shred it. Trust me when I tell you, it is worth the time to look deeply at your history before you begin a journey that makes your future. Ask God to reveal things about your past that you may never have thought of before. You will be amazed at the things you discover about yourself.

Ask God to reveal things about your past that you may never have thought of before.

So… Get the paper out! Or if you're on a train right now, just use the margins or the 'Notes' section at the end of the chapter. It's okay to write in the book. Don't read any further until you wrestle with these questions and come up with some answers.

Look at the things that could have affected you and your self-esteem. When did you start dieting? Why? Where did things go wrong? What bad habits did you pick up along the way?

What specifically disappoints you about who you were, or are, as a woman or man?

What would you change? What do you desire for your life?

Describe yourself at perfection. What do you see in the mirror?

As you peer into the future, how would you be living differently than you are now? What new habits would you have?

And what if you're not sure about God or if you can trust Him? That's okay too. Now may be a good time to ask God to reveal Himself to you as you read through this book.

The Bible says in 1 Chronicles 28:9, 'If you seek him, he will be found by you' and in Matthew 7: 7-8, 'Ask and it will be given to you; seek and you will find; knock and the door will be opened to you. For everyone who asks receives; he who seeks finds; and to him who knocks, the door will be opened.' God is a keeper of His word. If you want to develop a relationship with God, I promise He will be there to meet you every step of the way.

God is not a respecter of persons, meaning it doesn't matter who you are or what you have done, he loves you just the same because He created you. He will treat you with the same respect and gentleness as He does for all of his children. His deepest desire is for you to lay down your ideas of Him so He may show you the real truth, in order for you to begin a relationship with Him.

No one likes to begin a relationship with someone who has preconceived ideas of who you are and is not willing to give you a chance to be the real you. God loves you. All trust is developed over time so I do not expect you to just jump in all at once. Question God, search Him out and ask that He come and meet with you. Trust me, He can handle it, in fact, He looks forward to it!

'Trapped'

Is there no way to escape?

I'm trapped inside a life I do not want to lead, in a body I do not want. I've tried many times to break the barriers but as I near the border, it's the inside I 'need'.

My mind tricks me into thinking I cannot survive outside these walls. I believe and I crumble, back into the pit I nearly dug myself out of and I'm at the beginning once again.

The clear voices once heard outside are now just a mumble. I've been through this vicious cycle so many times. I scream out for help but no one hears; more than once I nearly died.

I hear him laugh and I almost let him win. The dark seems so powerful and causes so many fears. I can just barely see light, a faint glimmer in the dark, solemn night. Sometimes I can't see it at all but I know it's there. It's the only thing that gives me courage to fight.

Will I ever make it out of this alive? Why can't I just let go?

To be free and fly again, like I did once before; to discover and live in a world that holds life. Oh, if I could only break these walls I would know the answer.

It's so simple yet desires are so strong. (It's a battle). The mind says one thing but the body does not follow. The heart belongs to the light but the rest waivers between right and wrong. It requires me to give up my own will and desire and to follow. The dark calls this a sacrifice yet only when I follow I will be free.

Marla Jones
(written one year before she found freedom)

23

Notes:

24

Chapter Three
Temptation

N ow the Lord God had planted a garden in the east, in Eden; and there he put the man he had formed. And the Lord God made all kinds of trees grow out of the ground - trees that were pleasing to the eye and good for food. In the middle of the garden were the tree of life and the tree of the knowledge of good and evil.

The Lord God took the man and put him in the Garden of Eden to work it and take care of it. And the Lord God commanded the man, 'You are free to eat from any tree in the garden; but you must not eat from the tree of the knowledge of good and evil, for when you eat of it you will surely die.'

Genesis 2:8-9, 15-17

Imagine what it must have been like to live in the Garden of Eden. Actually, it is probably beyond what we could imagine; a garden that flourished with life. I don't imagine that it would *need* any maintenance, however the Lord must have known that man needed something to keep him amused so He created the garden to be just enough for Adam to work it and take care of it. Similar to many gardeners today, he must have found such satisfaction in a garden that was so beautiful and flourishing with life.

It bore fruit, vegetables and probably had food that we have never experienced. Adam and Eve had every nutrient they needed to keep them in perfect health. I don't imagine that there would be any poisonous plants or itchy grass. Adam and Eve did not have to worry about sinus medication or allergies to particular foods. The river watering the garden would be crystal clear and need no treatment or purification. The food would be all organic, natural-no pesticides, preservatives or additives. All things would be genetically modified by God himself.

In fact, the only thing mentioned that would not have benefited Adam and Eve was the fruit of the tree that God told them to keep away from.

'And the Lord God commanded the man, 'You are free to eat from any tree in the garden; but you must not eat from the tree of the knowledge of good and evil, for when you eat of it you will surely die.''
Genesis 2:16

Now, let's put ourselves in the Garden of Eden. Which part of the garden do you think you would have focused on? Would you focus on all the amazing things that you could eat, the beauty of the garden and an amazing relationship with the creator of everything or on the one thing that was off limits?

Choice offers the opportunity for genuine love.

In your life, do you see all the blessings in and around you or do you focus on the limited number of problems you are experiencing? Are you so focused on getting your weight under control that you have forgotten all the many good things in your life?

Over time, one negative thought or experience fed with questions, doubts and time dwelling upon it will consume any human. This is part of human nature, a part that separates us from God; yet it requires us to depend on God. We cannot defeat it on our own. But, you may be thinking, 'I want to do the right thing but I can't stop myself from giving into temptation; I desperately want to live a normal life and enjoy all the things life has to offer, it just seems impossible.' God did not have to create that tree. So why did he?

The creation of the tree shows the very heart and nature of God. God could have created robotic-like people that said that they loved God and did everything He commanded but what sort of a relationship is that? God desires to have a loving relationship with His people, His children. God loves you so much and His greatest desire is that you would truly fall in love with Him. But He certainly will not force you to love Him.

Choice offers the opportunity for genuine love. Having the choice to commit your heart to someone or to just walk away offers great freedom. When a person lovingly commits to another out of their own heart's desire, it means more than anything. Just ask anyone who is engaged to be married.

Writers have tried for centuries to pen into stories, poems and songs the definition of such true love. God's hope is that you would desire to get to know Him and to do what He asks as an act of showing your love for Him not out of a sense of fear or duty. God always gives us a choice. I do want to emphasize here that God created choice but not temptation. It is in our mind that we decide if something is a temptation or not.

So what is temptation? Take some time to define this word.

What does it mean in your life? A dictionary meaning doesn't define a word for the individual; it just gives a broad definition. So take some time to really think about it and discuss it with others, rather than look it up in a dictionary.

Temptation is

I think of temptations as a longing for something you shouldn't have. Having a deep desire for something that you just know isn't good for you. Wanting what is 'off-limits', wanting to do something naughty. It is different than a desire because we have some desires that are good, like to be married one day or to be the best at what we do, for example. The Bible says to delight yourself in the Lord and he will give you the desires of your heart (Psalm 37:4).

So temptation seems to have a negative after-effect attached to it. Not many people would say, for example, 'Ooh, I am so tempted to read the Bible today!' It would not be temptation if you were allowed to do it! There are many ways of describing it but each definition seems to come to the same conclusion-something about it is just not right.

Temptation is unique to each person yet common to all mankind. What this means is that what may tempt me, may not tempt you but temptation, in itself, makes its way into all of our lives in one way or another. It is highly personal and if discovered, most likely, would be very embarrassing. At the very heart of temptation is a very deceiving evil. When we encounter temptation, the Holy Spirit's flags go up in our conscience telling us that something is awry in our thinking but over time we are worn down either by the devil or our own fleshly thoughts continually telling us to ignore the Holy Spirit until we are no longer aware of the warning signs.

Temptation in itself is not a sin. Even Jesus was tempted by the devil.

Then Jesus was led by the Spirit into the desert to be tempted by the devil.

Matthew 4:1

Temptation is merely the bait. You are free of it until the bite is taken and then you are hooked. Once a decision is made to follow that temptation, then sin enters into the scene. It's like the spark before the fire, leading to struggles, heartache and pain.

Overcoming temptation becomes very tricky, as it requires you to put aside any pride you may have in yourself or your accomplishments and basically bare all to God. This is so hard to do, especially for those who feel they have never experienced God's love. There is a side of you that argues strongly, 'Why should I?' or 'I don't want to!' But how can you examine something if it is kept in the dark, where you hide all of these issues away.

The first key to overcoming temptation is to know exactly what your temptations are. List your temptations on a sheet of paper so you may bring them into the light, so to speak. Try and think beyond just food-related temptations. Take the time and look into every area of your life. List anything that pops into your mind even if it seems irrelevant at the time. Be specific and truthful as you look at your temptations, no matter how embarrassing it is for yourself.

As hard as this is, I believe if you can get it out on paper you may begin to examine them clearly, the way God wants you to see them. You will find that they are not as daunting as the devil would have you to believe. Pray for God's guidance as you do this exercise. I promise the painful part is bringing yourself to do this. Once your temptations are out there, your weaknesses exposed and your embarrassments clearly laid before him, you will experience what God calls 'grace' and it is the sweetest thing this side of heaven!

Here are some examples of what may be a temptation just to get you thinking.

* Being jealous of a friend's lifestyle- car, house, clothes, etc.
* Wanting a romantic encounter with someone outside of your marriage
* Just putting one last bet on.
* Eating or drinking that which is not healthy for you or beyond a healthy limit.
* Telling lies, big or small.
* Stealing from someone or cheating him of something due to him.
* Wanting something that you do not currently have in such a way that controls your life.

I strongly urge you again to pray for God to show you any 'hidden temptations' as there may be temptations in your life that are not obvious to you. I would venture to say that these are sometimes the most dangerous. If you have never prayed to God before, that's okay, just simply talk to Him like you would to anyone else. You may simply want to say, 'Lord, even though I'm not sure where all this is going please make me aware of any temptation in my life that may be a danger to me. Amen.'

Write down anything that comes to your mind, even if it doesn't make complete sense at the time, as God may reveal it's meaning at a later stage.

Temptations:

I believe this is where a line is drawn for many non-Christians and Christians alike. People believe that because God is holy and they have heard he will judge each person, they are afraid to lay their bare sin before him; afraid he will judge them and turn them away.

Even though I learn this lesson over and over, I speak from experience when I say that when you bring any sin, mistake, fault (whatever you want to call it) anything you are ashamed of before God, He will bring out the healing balm long before any gavel. His first priority is to heal you, cleanse you, and free you from the things that long to entrap you for life. The judgment we fear comes to anything **not** submitted to or under the authority of Jesus Christ.

This is what the 'good news' is all about. Yes, each one of us will experience God's judgment but those who have submitted their lives, sins, warts and all, will have Jesus as their representative – he will stand in for you. He is the first and only line of defense and that is all that anyone needs!

Now the serpent was more crafty than any of the wild animals the Lord God had made. He said to the woman, 'Did God really say; 'you must not eat from any tree in the garden'?'
The woman said to the serpent, 'We may eat fruit from the trees in the garden, but God did say, 'You must not eat fruit from the tree that is in the middle of the garden, and you must not touch it, or you will die'.

Genesis 3:1-3

In the Garden of Eden, Eve experienced the first temptation known to mankind. It's interesting that most portrayals of this scene from the Bible show Adam and Eve neatly fitted with fig leaves, sitting next to an apple tree, with a snake in the bottom corner. Eve has her arm gracefully draped above her as she is about to bring the apple to her mouth. Now why does the emphasis tend to be on the fruit? People wonder why she gave in so easily to something that they already had plenty of - food. Ah, but the food wasn't really the problem. The fruit was as relevant to Eve's problem as chocolate is to a person with a weight problem.

To people looking from the outside it may all look the same. They so easily say to the struggling dieter, 'Just stop eating chocolate or desert or (you fill in the blank) and you will lose weight' but to the dieter, who has probably heard that comment a thousand times, it offers absolutely no help at all. Dieters are not stupid people. They do know that eating deserts does not help their situation. Most of them are even cluey enough to know what is good for them, a well-balanced diet, exercise, etc. But making life changes, dealing with problems dug deep into the heart and discovering things about themselves that they may not like are not as easy as an off-the-cuff cliché.

Dieters are not stupid.

What lay behind Eve's decision to give into temptation? She may have been questioning if what God said was really the truth compared to what the serpent was saying. She may have been imagining what it would be like to have knowledge of good and evil, to be like God. Maybe it turned into a challenge, could she get away with this without God knowing? And so what if he did? Would he really follow through with what he said? Was it like the lotto where she hoped to win the total jackpot: 'I can live in the Garden of Eden and be like God too'?

What thoughts must have been pouring through her head as she debated back and forth in her mind over whether or not to challenge God's authority? Probably very similar thoughts to our own, when making similar decisions to give into what our body wants, craves, desires. Do we give in or follow a predetermined mindset to stay on the straight and narrow path - going in the right direction, doing the right thing? Surely one piece of fruit won't hurt me?

No matter what thought pattern she followed, Eve began the process of reasoning. She didn't just put the words of the serpent out of her mind, she entertained them, even romanticized them. I find it interesting that she did not discuss what the serpent said with God; to just flat out ask God 'is this true'? In fact, I just find it very interesting that she was even comfortable enough to be talking with a serpent, therefore allowing his opinion to be validated.

The more you think upon temptation, the more it will have a hold on you. The more you venture along this path, the more alluring the unknown behind the temptation becomes. Unfortunately if you travel too far down this path it is very difficult to find your way back. With each step you take you become more and more numb to any sort of warning from God. You begin to reason with the truth and excuses begin to take the place of wisdom. The path behind you seems to disappear into the darkness. This is why Jesus is called the light of the world. He shines through that darkness to show us to the path He originally intended us to travel upon.

Eve may have reasoned with herself that she wasn't guilty of sin as there is no record of God speaking directly to her about the tree of good and evil. Eve received the warning of the tree second hand through Adam. But judging from the words that were stated to the serpent, she did know what God had said and understood its meaning.

I bring this point up only because Eve is very similar to all humans today in that God may not speak to us directly about an issue but we have His word given to us in the Bible. Yes, it is secondhand through the people God chose to use but, none the less, its meaning and truth still remain. We are still held accountable to His word and His commands whether or not we choose to read or follow them.

'...but you must not eat from the tree of the knowledge of good and evil, for when you eat of it you will surely die.'

Genesis 2:17

'When the woman saw that the fruit of the tree was good for food and pleasing to the eye, and also desirable for gaining wisdom, she took some and ate it. She also gave some to her husband, who was with her, and he ate it.'

Genesis 3:6

Compare Genesis 2:17 with Genesis 3:6. The tree has not changed but Eve's vision of the tree has. The visualization of temptation is one of the keys to its success. It seems to make your vision change somehow. It's as if the more you think about it the more it has a hold of you.

Read Genesis 2:17 again. If you were told that your piece of chocolate mud cake contained enough poison to be lethal and if you were to eat it you would surely die, how would you visualize your piece of mud cake?

If I were to set a tray of an assortment of beautiful foods before you and told you that each food contained malaria or HIV cells, how would your view change from the original image you had?

Well the devil managed to alter Eve's view considerably by the time we get to Genesis 3:4-6. The tree hasn't changed at all here. The very same tree that God said would surely kill Adam and Eve if they touched it was now, 'good for food and pleasing to the eye, and also desirable for gaining wisdom,' (Genesis 3:6).

35

What is your view of the temptations lying before you? For example, when I would see a diet from a magazine and the beautiful model next to it, in my mind I would visualize myself at the perfect weight, living free and fitting into all of my clothes. My life would be perfect and I would be happy and problem free. I could begin a new life.

As great as that would sound, that's a lot of expectation to place on a single diet thrown into a magazine somewhere. Yet it would fill me with hope and off I would go, the problem being when I failed and faltered because the diet became too hard to follow. I would give up and give in and gain more weight again, tunneling into a pit of depression.

Realistically, if I had examined my view closely before beginning the diet, warning flags should have gone up. Life will never be perfect and there is no diet that will fix all your problems. You will never look like that particular model and, honestly, why would you want to? You are a beautiful creation of God! It's time to live your life and not hers. And why wait for the completion of a diet to start living life? Start living now. Start doing the things now that you frequently say you'll get around to doing 'one day'. By addressing the problems in your spiritual realm first, the physical appearance will adjust accordingly.

Altering that view is another key to success but we cannot alter that view alone. Pray for God's vision on everything. View some of the temptations before you from a different angle and write how they look from a different perspective.

The interesting thing about the deception found in temptation is that there is always a hint of good or truth in it; otherwise you wouldn't fall for it. Giving into temptation will, most likely, feel fantastic for a time but unfortunately, the time is so short and at the end of it one manages to somehow get lost, feel isolated, lonely or depressed. It is during this time the devil will try to make it look like the deception lies in the heart of God and will try to turn your anger and failure towards God in a blaming manner.

Look closely again at Genesis 3:4, 5. There was a bit of truth in what the devil said. Adam and Eve did not die, at least not immediately or in the physical way they thought. And they certainly did acquire some knowledge but this was not the 'wisdom' that Eve desired in verse 6.
Godly wisdom is very different than just having knowledge. Knowledge is filled with information whereas wisdom is what you do with it. Godly wisdom is doing the right thing with this information and only God can give us this type of wisdom.

When we operate in the wisdom of God, we experience the fruits of the spirit listed in Galatians 5:22, love, joy, peace, patience, kindness, goodness, faithfulness, gentleness and self-control. When we operate in our own wisdom we only end up feeling disappointed and discouraged.

I wonder if things would have been different if Eve could have humbly brought her thoughts of disobeying God's command before Him and asked for help.

As we look at the consequences of their choice to eat the fruit the difference between knowledge and wisdom become clear. First they realized they were naked (knowledge) and this was not a good feeling. Then they went immediately to work to cover up their bodies - sound familiar?

This wisdom is from themselves rather than God. Then, when God comes into the garden, they go into hiding. Listen to the words that stand out in the next few passages… 'naked, hid, afraid, deceived, cursed, painful toil, thorns, thistles, sweat, return to dust, banished…' I don't know about you but that kind of wisdom I can certainly do without!

Short-term consequences involved pain and heart ache. The long-term consequence was a death sentence they never would have acquired if they had not had their view of truth distorted. How hard it is to accept that we are only human, with limited knowledge, dependent on God. We are so easily deceived that we can do all things on our own. But when we fail, we don't want to take responsibility for our own mistakes. Even Adam and Eve do not take responsibility for their own actions, blaming each other and then blaming the serpent. Although it's not mentioned, I am sure that after being banished from the garden, Adam and Eve were even blaming God.

I wonder if things would have been different if Eve could have humbly brought her thoughts of disobeying God's command before Him and asked for help. If she had only given him a chance to reply to the questions and doubts the devil had put into her head, I'm sure she would have found that God would not have just turned away from her.

Can we bring our thoughts before him now before we get too entangled in our own deception of temptation?

Imagine what your life would be like if you gave into your temptations continually. Despite what the devil would have you believe, you would be miserable! But it is so hard to imagine it could be anything less than perfect. Maybe someone else's temptation, but mine? No! But if you have ever given into any temptation you will know exactly what I mean.

Go back to Genesis chapter 3 and outline all the consequences of Adam and Eve's decisions.

Now outline all the consequences you would face if you gave into the temptations you have previously listed. So, how do we escape the temptations that lie before us? Pray!

Consequences to my sin:

'Pray so that you will not fall into temptation,'
Matthew 26:41

God is the standard to which the human race can measure what is good and bad. The world will tell you that everything is good or that anything is bad depending on the day. Much of the worldly wisdom is based on feeling. Do whatever *feels* right. The problem with this is that feelings are continually changing.

God is the only rock upon which feelings can be anchored into. He is unchanging. He was the same throughout history and He continues to remain the same today. God will forever be the same. This is such a comfort in an ever changing world. With the conviction of the Holy Spirit and the knowledge of the living word of God you will be able to determine immediately if what lies before you is good for you, or if it is a temptation (remember a temptation is not good for you).

As soon as it becomes a temptation, in the most immediate sense, run! Run to God because He cannot be tempted by evil (according to James 1:13). Let it go and do not entertain the thoughts of the temptation. Realize that if you want more, then you are not completely fulfilled in Christ, so return to Him and find your completeness in Him. Nothing in this world will satisfy the empty longing and yearning in your soul, only Jesus Christ can fill the void. Once you come to grips with this, no temptation will be able to have a hold of you.

Read and meditate on the word of God. Jesus defeated the devil's temptations in the desert by stating God's word. Go back and have a read for yourself in Matthew 4. By using God's word you not only resist the devil but you learn more about God. By focusing on the truths of the Bible, you get your focus off the temptation and off of yourself.

Satan has worked so hard to create a pattern for women and men to constantly try and fit into. He has immersed all media with it and filled minds with it. The Bible says 'Do not conform any longer to the pattern of this world but be transformed by the renewing of your mind,' Romans 12:2-3.

Did you notice that Adam and Eve did not struggle with self-image problems in the Garden of Eden prior to eating the forbidden fruit? Adam and Eve would have had perfect self-confidence in who they were as people. Genesis 2:25 states they were without shame. Any questions or doubts that arose would have faded quickly as they conversed with God daily. The wonder and awe of walking with God would give them perfect peace. They would experience joy and contentment just knowing they were created in God's image. They truly were perfect in every way.

Can you imagine being in a place like the Garden of Eden? Even if not physically living in the garden, just being at a place where you are completely comfortable with who you are and who God created you to be? Understanding your purpose in life and knowing that you are perfect in every way to God? What things do you think would change about the way you live life? Would you be happy?

The whole issue of weight is a battle for your mind. The way you look can consume your entire being without you even being aware of it. Really listen to the conversations between women and men around you. I think you will be shocked at how much of it revolves around what foods one should or should not have or who is trying a new diet, switching diets or quitting diets.

If the devil can make you feel defeated, hopeless, lost, angry and upset and turn your focus entirely on you and your failure - what more does he have to do than convince you that you are ugly, fat, and worthless? For the majority of men and women, he knows just where to place his target.

Unfortunately, most weight loss programs teach that you are in control of your body and your life and that if you fail, it is due to your lack of self-discipline.

I think the issue of dieting has been long overlooked as a spiritual issue. People think 'relationship with God' is a completely separate issue to 'my diet and the way I look'. Unfortunately, most weight loss programs teach that you are in control of your body and your life and that if you fail, it is due to your lack of self-discipline. They only focus on the diet plan and the physical results, not even scraping the surface to find out what is at the core. God wants to go deeper and let you know there is a bigger plan and His heart's desire is for you to find freedom from ever dieting again.

Notes:

Chapter Four
The Core

Imagine you are at an expensive cocktail party for a very important function. Notable people from every walk of life are there, including a few celebrities and even some royalty. Everyone is busy with introductions and chatting about various topics of interest. As you approach the door to enter, the host of the party introduces you. 'This is Sue. She is five foot seven, weighs a whopping hundred and ninety three pounds and wears a size twenty six and a half.'

What would be your next words? I think the only words said would be 'Are you alright?' to the host, a few minutes after he has been lying on the floor knocked out by Sue!

We do not introduce ourselves according to our physical appearance or measurements because that is not who we are. We are more than just flesh, blood, bone and water. We have roles, hobbies, interests, ideas and character. It is the inner being that people want to get to know and love.

I am made up of many things. In my roles, I am a daughter and a mother, a sister and a friend. I am a wife and a lover. I am a learner and an educator. I love to invent and to write. I do crafts and I do housework. Occasionally, I delve into finances and home maintenance. There are many things that make up who I am.

What are the things that make up who you are? What is in the core of the physical shell?

There are many roles we play in life and there are many characteristics that make up our personality. We get to know each other beyond just mere acquaintance by discovering what lies behind the physical appearance. As people get to know you, this is how they literally begin to see you. Yes, they see the physical outer shell but it starts to dim the more they come to know who you really are.

We do not introduce ourselves according to our physical appearance or measurements because that is not who we are.

The physical fades to a point that it is barely noticed in a healthy relationship. Often, it takes quite an effort to notice even a change in hair styles. Think about your friends. If I asked you to tell me about them, would you just describe their physical appearance? The physical is just so shallow. I only write this to let you know that you are your harshest critic. Apart from an abusive relationship, no one criticizes you as hard as you do. (Note: if you are in an abusive relationship you need to seek professional help immediately).

We see the physical shell of a person first and then move in to get to know the personality, intellect and emotions of a person. If we become very good friends with a person, we may even discover some of the issues that lay deep within the heart of a person. Often, however, those deep issues are rarely disclosed to anyone, even good friends.

God works in exactly the opposite direction of a man. He looks immediately to the core issues within the heart and then works his way out. 1 Samuel 16:7 states '...The Lord does not look at the things man looks at. Man looks at the outward appearance, but the Lord looks at the heart.' The physical is the last thing the Lord sees. Think back to the Garden of Eden, did the Lord express shock at their nakedness? No, He addressed the other issues first and then clothed them just before they left the garden. He clothed them for their peace of mind, not His.

God's view of man is so different to the way we think and view other people. The physical shell that seems to hold so much value to man, is simply dust formed by God in a day. And there it will return when we leave this earth. It is a temporary body that will be replaced by a heavenly body one day. The various identities of who you really are and your personality characteristics form somewhat of an outward physical appearance to God.

Now the things you did not write down, the deep heart issues that you rarely, if ever, tell anyone about, these are the things that God sees on the inside of the 'physical'. He knows you best on this level. And if you are a Christian, at the very core of your being, he sees himself. This is what salvation is all about. When people invite Christ into their lives, he dwells deep within the heart of man. And instead of seeing all of the sin and evil in your life he sees himself and thereby is able to commune with you; holy with unholy, made holy by Christ.

This is why God is so interested in healing the inner issues first, because what is within bubbles out onto the surface. Sometimes when I observe a person in absolute worship of God they appear as if they are glowing. The inward transforms the outer. On a surface level that is how we can see if someone is in a fantastic mood because it just radiates out. Likewise if something is wrong it also will manage to express itself in the facial expressions and body language of a person.

If something is wrong for a long time the physical begins to wear down from the stress of these problems and many times we develop physical ailments ranging from a common cold to severe migraine headaches. We may also develop emotional ailments like depression. This can lead to lack of sleep and irregular eating patterns which in turn lead to more physical and emotional problems. If we are not careful, this cycle can take us down a very destructive path.

God's greatest desire, once invited to dwell within the core of a person, is to line up all the layers, including the deepest innermost desires, our roles in life and our physical appearance, to him. When this happens we begin to experience the complete joy, peace, freedom, contentment and holiness that make up the very nature of God. God contains everything we need for perfect health in our body, mind and soul. We just cannot accomplish this perfect alignment on our own because we are not perfect- we are not God.

In an artistic view, God has set a mould through the imprint of his son Jesus so we may be transformed into his likeness. Jesus came to this earth and lived the same life every human lives yet he did it perfectly, setting the mould of how it is meant to be done. He completely submitted His life to the will of God, the Father. We can not live like Jesus without depending on God to make and mould us into His image.

The material that God works with is our hearts. The problem is that most moulds require very pliable material so that they may be set properly. Our hearts determine our pliability. Depending on the condition of our heart, God has to work with all types of material, some even like concrete. Because concrete just does not easily pour into a mould it may need to be chiseled away at over time or sometimes it may need to be broken. So many times we think the Lord leaves us in the tough times, when really he is breaking things away we have desperately clung onto, thinking those things would save us, instead of relying on the only one who can truly save us.

Even when the material is pliable, the shape of Jesus' mould feels so abnormal at first. There is nothing like it in this world.

Everything Jesus said and did was the opposite of what the world was teaching. Jesus said,

'If the world hates you, keep in mind that it hated me first. If you belonged to the world, it would love you as its own. As it is, you do not belong to the world, but I have chosen you out of the world.'
John 15:18, 19

Do not love the world or anything in the world. If anyone loves the world, the love of the Father is not in him. For everything in the world-the cravings of sinful man, the lust of his eyes and the boasting of what he has and does-comes not from the Father but from the world. The world and its desires pass away, but the man who does the will of God lives forever.   1 John 2:15-17

We are to be in the world but not of the world. When we are being transformed by God into the likeness of his son, it feels as if someone is trying to fit an octopus into the mould of a canary. Our sinful nature is just resistant to the holy nature of God. The good news is that God doesn't just force us into this mould against our resistant will and sensitive emotions. Once we have invited God into to our lives to change us to what He desires, he gently softens us over time through various struggles and situations until the mould begins to feel more comfortable. Eventually the mould becomes not only comfortable but enjoyable and we wonder why we ever resisted so hard before.

When Samuel thought he had found the next king of the land because of his strong appearance the Lord said:

'Do not consider his appearance or his height for I have rejected him. The Lord does not look at the things man looks at. Man looks at the outward appearance, but the Lord looks at the heart,'
1 Samuel 16:7

We are all capable of making judgements based on first impressions but if we can't move on from that in maturity to get to know someone, we miss out on a lot of rewarding relationships. If Samuel had not listened to God, he would have anointed King David's brother to be the next king instead of David. He would have missed getting to know David, the great man of God. People who continue to judge others based on physical appearance never experience the rewards that come from deep, meaningful relationships and that is very sad.

Without relationships, what else is there to enjoy in life? Now may be a good time to examine what else is in your life. When you look at your days in general, what do you spend most of your time doing? So much of what we do is just busyness; doing things that will need to be done again and again, over and over.

Probably one of the most irritating things I experience is spending an entire day cleaning the house only to have it look exactly the same the next day. The most annoying chore to me is doing the dishes because just when you think you are finished, another mealtime arrives and out they come again. You really realize how much our lives revolve around food when you are the one who does the dishes. I just feel like I am never finished, ever.

I remember watching a show on television a while ago where they took couples and families from modern day households and challenged them to live out on the prairie for a year. The families were excited to try a new adventure building their own log cabins to live in, growing food from the land and looking after animals. They were a self-sustaining group of people basically living in the middle of nowhere.

I will never forget the last days of the experiment when they interviewed each family member about his or her experience. One woman standing in the kitchen said something like: 'Basically you are looking at where I've been for the whole year, standing in this blasted kitchen! Either I've been cooking or preparing to cook or cleaning up after I cook. I thought this would be an adventure living out in the wild and getting back to nature, when all I've experienced is what I do at home just made harder'. As you can imagine, she was very excited to get back into the modern world.

The book of Ecclesiastes describes this feeling of never getting anywhere. Solomon starts this book with the statement that everything is meaningless.

In Ecclesiastes 1:9, he goes on to say: 'What has been will be again, what has been done will be done again; there is nothing new under the sun'. Basically his point is that there is nothing that can't be traced back to history somewhere. Sure there are new ways of doing old habits - technology has insured that - but for all the technology we have, why are our lives still busy, still filled with sorrow and unhappiness? Should we not have 'evolved' into the happiest human beings by now?

He continues with such wisdom (remember Solomon was deemed the wisest man ever to live).

'A man can do nothing better than to eat and drink and find satisfaction in his work. This too, I see, is from the hand of God, for without him, who can eat or find enjoyment? To the man who pleases him, God gives wisdom, knowledge and happiness, but to the sinner he gives the task of gathering and storing up wealth to hand it over to the one who pleases God. This too is meaningless, a chasing after the wind.'

Ecclesiastes 2:24-26

What are your goals in life?

Many people struggle to earn money and lots of it. I agree with Solomon when he says:

'Whoever loves money never has money enough; whoever loves wealth is never satisfied with his income,'

Ecclesiastes 5:10

I have met a few very wealthy and rich people and it is sad to see that even with all that they have acquired in life they are still very unhappy people. In fact they are so unhappy, that they tend to make everyone around them unhappy too. Now, I personally think it is fantastic to be wealthy but true contentment is something that only God can give. One of the most famous sayings Job cried out in his hardships is this:

'Naked a man comes from his mother's womb, and as he comes, so he departs. He takes nothing from his labour that he can carry in his hand.' Job 1:21

You've probably heard it said a hundred different ways. 'You can't take it with you when you die.' or 'The man with the most toys still dies'. So, if you come into the world with nothing and you leave with nothing, what will you invest your time and energy into?

The things that you put the most time and energy into are the things you value the most. If you can imagine a clock with 24 hours on it, what do you fill the hours with? What do you do with the time given to you? Maybe now is a good time to just list the top 10 priorities in your life.

You may need to have two lists, one in principle and one in practical, because we do not always live the way we think we do in our minds.

For example, I may say spending time with my family is a top priority, however if I look at the amount of time I realistically spend with my family, maybe it is not as high of a priority as I thought. What I desire may not be what is actually happening in my life.

Don't forget to mention where food and self-image fit into your lists.

Top Priorities in Principle   Top Priorities Realistically

_____   _____

_____   _____

_____   _____

_____   _____

_____   _____

_____   _____

_____   _____

_____   _____

Here is another tough question. If you had to sum up the purpose of your life in a sentence, what would it be? Why are you here on this earth?

_____

_____

That is the challenge, fitting your life purpose on that one line!

Carl Jung once said, 'If you don't know who you are, then the world will tell you.' How true this is! I look at so many people trying to live up to what the media says is the way to live and I feel sorry for them. They will never be able to attain what the perfect

52

image is because the perfect image is a mirage. When you get close to it you realize there is nothing there. It was all a deception. Others are always trying to live up to the standards placed on them by friends, family and even people they barely know!

The problem is that so many differing opinions and expectations are confusing. How can you ever feel the satisfaction of reaching the goals of who you are meant to be when your goals change everyday, depending on who you are trying to please? Do you know who you are? What is the image of yourself based on? Is it dictated by what others tell you or on what you know to be true?

I encourage you to take time out with God, as much time as it takes, and really refine your purpose into one sentence; not a paragraph or a page. After you refine it, memorize it! Once you really know what your purpose is, then you stop struggling to define who you are and what you should be doing. You attain peace because you know where you are going. Everyone is so busy in our world, most being too busy. But when you are living with purpose you no longer overcommit yourself to everything because if it doesn't line up with your purpose, you won't feel guilty about saying 'no'; a problem so many people struggle with.

If you don't know who you are, then the world will tell you.

Finally, what thoughts do you fill your head with throughout the day? In the last 24 hours, what thoughts have consumed your mind? Are they positive thoughts or self-condemning thoughts?

Having thought about food and body image mainly all day, everyday, the first real struggle I had was wondering what to think or do now that I was finished with dieting. It was only when I stopped to evaluate just how much food consumed each day of my life that I realized what a grip it had on me.

From the moment I woke up, I was thinking: 'What will I eat today? I wonder if I can just stick to my plan and eat healthy for just one day. What will I wear? What can I wear? What will hide the most flaws?'

Then came the self-condemning thoughts like, 'If you weren't such a pig you could get into that outfit or even shop for clothes!' Nothing in the shops seemed to fit. (And those mirrors in the change room! How much more condemnation can one take? They show full frontal and rear views under florescent lights!)

I would look at other women who were thin and wonder how they stayed that way. Sometimes I would try and copy everything they did, so maybe I would turn out like them. If I wasn't thinking about weight, I was feeling it. I felt heavy, lethargic, slow and depressed.

I would end each day rethinking the last 24 hours, upset at my lack of 'will power' (an interesting concept, who's will is it and is it any wonder why it doesn't really have any power at all?) and trying to just gather hope for one more day.

I think it is the very first diet that sets you up for this horrible cycle that just keeps tumbling downward. I wish I could put warning labels on diets like they have on the cigarette packs. Warning! This diet causes a very addictive habit of dieting and can be fatal to your health.

The first diet sets the trap up so well because it works well, too well! It sets you up for a very deceptive future. You always seem to remember the success of that first diet and

We are very good at over-commitment, which really is not commitment at all.

54

that is what seems to push you on; motivating you enough to try, try again. But most of the diets following that glowing first review are not so easy. Your body has now adjusted to storing up fat for the next starvation time. It doesn't want to lose weight so easily any more. You become tired of it mentally – 'Here we go again' is the predominant thought. You eventually give up until something or someone comes along and hurts you enough to attempt it again.

We have pondered upon life's hardest questions. Summed up, they basically ask; 'Who are you?' and 'Where are you going?' If you do not know the answer to these questions, you open yourself to be blown about by the world's constant wind of change and confusion. It becomes much easier to discard anything that does not line up with your purpose for living, when you know exactly who you are and where you are going. Doubt and confusion can not get a grip on you like it may have previously.

Jesus said, 'No one can serve two masters. Either he will hate the one and love the other, or he will be devoted to the one and despise the other. You cannot serve both God and Money.'   Matthew 6:24

Would you say that you are totally committed to anything or anyone? Besides taking responsibility for our actions, I think commitment is one of the hardest things our society struggles with. We are very good at over-commitment, which really is not commitment at all.

Notice that this verse does not say 'you cannot serve God and have money'. It says that you cannot **serve** both God and money. The difference is the act of servanthood. God does not mind if you have money, He does not want you to be controlled by it. Jesus had enough money to warrant the need of Judas as his treasurer, yet notice who became the slave to money. Judas sold out on Jesus for thirty silver coins. Listen to how the story ends.

'When Judas, who had betrayed him, saw that Jesus was condemned, he was seized with remorse and returned the thirty silver coins to the chief priests and the elders. 'I have sinned,' he said, 'for I have betrayed innocent blood.'

'What is that to us?' they replied. 'That's your responsibility.' So Judas threw the money into the temple and left. Then he went away and hanged himself.'   Matthew 27:3-5

This is a striking example of how servanthood to money can quickly turn into slavery to money. God knows the power that money, and other things equivalent to it, can have over us and he wants to spare us the pain and consequences they leave in their path. But in order to spare you, he requires that you choose whom you will serve.

What is a servant?

Granted, it is hard to think about what this role means today in our society, because there are not many servants who serve a 'master' as such. Let's think what the role of a servant would be in context to a king.

I imagine if the king called, the servant would drop everything and go. He would do anything to please the king. In fact, his whole life would revolve around what the king did and said. A servant would not have any rights, because merely being in that role would mean foregoing any rights. Your thoughts would be filled with everything from knowing the king's schedule to knowing his likes and dislikes, even trying to pre-empt what he may want next in order to please him. On the negative side, disobeying the king or even questioning his authority could lead to life imprisonment or even death.

Many people are afraid to give their lives to God because they think He wants to take everything away from them. They have heard you have to give up anything that is fun and give all your money to the church. That is not what Jesus has in mind at all. He says, 'I have come to give life and give it abundantly'.

Coming to a heavenly king is similar in some ways to coming to an earthly king. We know he has the power to allow us to live or die. We really have nothing to offer him that he doesn't already have save our very lives. But without his blessing our lives become very difficult. In fact, if he doesn't find favor with us, that's pretty much the end of the line. Where does one go or what does one do next if the king's acceptance is absent? We come virtually naked before him.

The book of Esther is an excellent example of what it means to approach an earthly king. Esther's brother Mordecai persuaded Esther to approach the king to save her people. Listen to the agonizing in her words:

'All the king's officials and the people of the royal provinces know that for any man or woman who approaches the king in the inner court without being summoned the king has but one law: that he be put to death. The only exception to this is for the king to extend the gold scepter to him and spare his life,'

Esther 4:11

When you approach a king you take your very life in with you. We come before the throne bowing down, hoping the king will extend the scepter to us, knowing we will remain a servant to him until the day we die. Here is where the analogy changes. With God we come humbly before him as a servant but instead of extending the scepter he extends his hand and lifts us up calling us his son or daughter, an heir to his kingdom.

However, he does not make us an heir to his throne - He will always be the King, the one in control. Some people have difficulty in giving up to God what they think they have control over but I see it as having all the rights as a family member and access to all the heavenly treasure without having the responsibility of being in charge of it all. It seems to always come down to this control issue. What is it exactly, that you think you have control of?

The gifts God brings are the fruit of the spirit: *'love, joy, peace, patience, kindness, goodness, faithfulness, gentleness and self-control,'* (Galatians 5:22).

Paul says in Philippians 4:12, 'I know what it is to be in need, and I know what it is to have plenty. I have learned the secret of being content in any and every situation' When was the last time you could say that you were completely content and just plain happy? God teaches us the secret of contentment. God loves us for who we are and accepts us just the way we are, giving us the secret to find real freedom in the way we live.

Compare this to what the world has to offer. A lot of material stuff which once acquired leaves one wanting more or worrying about how to protect it, not to mention the business of looking after it. A friend of mine once said that people are so busy trying to create a paradise here on earth that they forget there is an eternal paradise already created, perfect in every way and virtually free, a gift to all those who can lay pride aside and accept it.

Now let's look at servanthood to money. There are many people who serve money whether they admit it or not. How many people would drop anything to earn a few bucks? Unfortunately, if offered enough money, many people would compromise their self worth and values. Many of the 'hidden' professions exist because of this. It's not as if little girls dream of being a prostitute one day or little boys who as a child say, 'I'm gonna grow up and work in the black market'.

The difference between serving and having money revolves around the hold it has upon you. Are you the type of person who is always thinking about what to buy next? Can you always find something you 'need' in the advertisements? If you were given enough food, drink and clothes to survive, could you not only survive but also be content in doing so?

I could ask the same questions in relation to dieting. Are you the type of person who is always thinking about what to eat next? Can you always find something you need to do in order to get to that perfect weight goal? Could you ever just be content with who you are now? Money and dieting are very similar in that you could serve both endlessly and never be satisfied.
In fact, the difference between serving and having anything in this life depends on the hold it has upon you. You could equally substitute many things in money's place. You cannot serve both God and diets, you cannot serve both God and your own self-image, you cannot serve both God and other people's opinions of you. Can you have them, yes but serve them, no.

'Everything is permissible - but not everything is beneficial. Everything is permissible for me - but I will not be mastered by anything.'   1 Corinthians 6:12

What things pull at your servanthood to God? (Or stop you from serving God all together?)

Many things stop us from serving God: misunderstanding, being too busy, thinking we are too far away from God for him to even want us, our own thoughts and self-condemnation, etc. I think one of the biggest blockages that stop us from serving God is worry.

Worry is:

As you did with temptation, define 'worry' in your own words.
Worry seems to weigh down a person. It happens when you don't
have an answer and you struggle to find solutions. Worry is a lack
of trust in a person, situation or God. It's like an inner tug-o-war
between reasoning and trust.

When it involves children, we worry if they will remember what
we have taught them or how they will respond to outside pressures.
Can we trust them to do the right thing?

When it comes to God, our worry is very similar. Is God really
who He says He is? Is He really in control of everything? Can we
trust an invisible God who loves us or do we try and use the
world's scientific theories to reason our way through problems?

When it comes to dieting and self-image a whole realm of issues
arise for the worrier. They involve health issues (diabetes, joint

problems, general well being), physical issues (will I be able to walk more than one block?), social issues (will people really love me for who I am or will they be so repulsed by what they see they won't take the chance to get to know me?) and dreams and goals (how can I do anything with my life if I can't even get my weight under control?). Just to be able to fit into the clothes in the wardrobe is enough to worry about.

Therefore I tell you, do not worry about your life, what you will eat or drink; or about your body, what you will wear. Is not life more important than food, and the body more important than clothes? Look at the birds of the air; they do not sow or reap or store away in barns, and yet your heavenly Father feeds them. Are you not much more valuable than they? Who of you by worrying can add a single hour to his life?

And why do you worry about clothes? See how the lilies of the field grow? Yet I tell you that not even Solomon in all his splendor was dressed like one of these. If that is how God clothes the grass of the field, which is here today and tomorrow is thrown into the fire, will he not much more clothe you, O you of little faith?

So do not worry, saying, 'What shall we eat?' or 'What shall we drink?' or 'What shall we wear?' For the pagans run after all these things, and your heavenly Father knows that you need them. But seek first his kingdom and his righteousness, and all these things will be given to you as well. Therefore do not worry about tomorrow, for tomorrow will worry about itself. Each day has enough trouble of its own.

Matthew 6:24-34

Which is more important to you, life or food? The purpose of food is to nourish our bodies in order that we may live life to the full. What is God's purpose for you? To give you life and have it to the full (see John 10:10). God promises a crown of life to those who love him. (see James 1:12).

Food is symbolic of what Jesus Christ is to the soul. He nourishes us and feeds us, giving us life. Yet food is only a symbol and cannot fulfill our deepest desires like Christ can. Here is where we can go wrong, if we try to use food to satisfy what only God can satisfy. Food will never do the job.

I find one of the best methods of combating worry, after spending quality time with God, is to focus on the best things in life and put more energy into thinking upon these things. The more we think and speak negatively, the more we depress ourselves and go spiraling downwards. The only way to start combating this downward spiral is to force yourself to think of something positive and start the spiral moving in the other direction.

What are the things that you enjoy doing the most? What things has God given you that you can truly rejoice in? List the blessings in your life; literally count your blessings. What are the good things that you have in your life? What are you thankful for?

Now hold this list up to the list of worries. Which do you want to start living for? Where was food and self-image in your thought patterns and priorities? Is food helping you live or are you living for food? Do you control it or does it control you? Most likely if you are reading this you are not in control. And the good news is that you don't have to be. God can control this and by relying on Him, he can stop it from controlling you. His desire is that you would not be a slave to anything but rather to be in a loving and lasting relationship with him. God loves you and wants to help you. As Matthew 6:33 states,

'Seek first his kingdom and all these things shall be added unto you.'

As we read above God does know what we need in order to be happy in life. This may be hard to imagine especially if you feel you are being crushed on every side. Where do you begin when you feel your life is falling apart and no one around you seems to understand? Can God really help me through problems that seem to consume my life?

Trust in the Lord with all your heart and lean not on your own understanding; in all your ways acknowledge him. And he will make your paths straight. Do not be wise in your own eyes; fear the Lord and shun evil. This will bring health to your body and nourishment to your bones.

Proverbs 3:5-8

Notes:

Chapter Five
Heartbreakers

I remember when I first met my close friend Jacqui. She invited me around to her house one afternoon for a cup of tea and a chat. I began to scan over all of the beautiful photos of her family around the room. As I began to focus in on them more, I recalled meeting her family at church. I had met two boys and her husband. Yet there was another family member in the photo I had not met, a little baby boy. As the conversation progressed I said to her: 'It is so quiet in your house; is your baby sleeping?'

She then proceeded to tell me how she and her husband so looked forward to the arrival of their third child yet days before the delivery date the doctors could not find a heartbeat of the little one in her womb. She then had to be induced and give birth to a child that had already left this earth. They had a 'family' photo taken together before burying the child. That was the photo that I had been admiring.

My heart just broke into pieces as she told the story. How awful it would have been to carry a child for the full nine months only to find out days before the Lord had already taken him home. Then to go through all the pain and agony of childbirth and have to face the reality of death, face to face.

There are many situations that I do not understand and so many more that absolutely wrench my heart. It seems there are so many people with stories of pain and hardships. All of which are simply heartbreaking.

What things have broken your heart? What are you holding onto from the past? There may be certain things you are going through right now that feel they are crushing you or things that you dread may one day happen to you. List the things that break or potentially could break your heart and write how you feel about these things.

I rarely ever watch television any more and although I have a huge conviction about not watching most TV programs, I do admit I still love to have the occasional 'veg out' time in front of a good show. Hence lies the problem, finding a good show. It seems that every channel shows things that upset me, make me angry or just break my heart (or lure me into viewing things I know that I should not watch).

The biggest show that I avoid is the nightly news. Even though I am interested in world affairs, I find that about ten stories into the program, I feel depressed and almost hopeless. Stories of war, hardships, persecutions, children suffering, people dying, senseless crime and terrorization just get to be too much. So many things break my heart: the loss of loved ones, hurtful words, children labelled or rejected, racism, betrayal, feeling helpless to help someone in need, cruelty to animals, being taken for granted, missed opportunities, failure, loneliness and isolation of the elderly, completely messing something up (especially with your children) and these are just to name a few.

Out of the many things in the world that break my heart, I would say the thing that gets to me the most is when I know I'm the cause of someone's broken heart. When I do the very thing I have told myself I will not do. When I miss out on the perfect opportunity to bless or help someone and instead I manage to mess it all up and make a situation, that I was trying to help, become much worse. It's hard enough to know others around me cause hardship but what about when I look in the mirror? What do I do when I am the cause of someone's broken heart? What can I do when I know that I can't even control the person residing within me?

Paul writes about the ongoing conflict within us, knowing what is right yet not being able to carry it out in our life. Can you relate? In Romans 7:14- 25 Paul writes:

We know that the law is spiritual; but I am unspiritual, sold as a slave to sin. I do not understand what I do. For what I want to do I do not do, but what I hate I do. And if I do what I do not want to do, I agree that the law is good.

As it is, it is no longer I myself who do it, but it is sin living in me. I know that nothing good lives in me, that is, in my sinful nature. For I have the desire to do what is good, but I cannot carry it out. For what I do is not the good I want to do; no, the evil I do not want to do - this I keep on doing. Now if I do what I do not want to do, it is no longer I who do it, but it is sin living in me that does it.

So I find this law at work; when I want to do good, evil is right there with me. For in my inner being I delight in God's law; but I see another law at work in the members of my body, waging war against the law of my mind and making me a prisoner of the law of sin at work within my members. What a wretched man (or woman) I am! Who will rescue me from this body of death? Thanks be to God - through Jesus Christ our Lord!

So then, I myself in my mind am a slave to God's law, but in the sinful nature a slave to the law of sin.

I think you either totally understand this passage or it just completely goes over your head. Sometimes I wish I didn't understand it so well! But I do love this passage of scripture because it makes me feel like finally someone understands! Coming from an eating disorder, I have lived this scripture out daily. I wanted so badly to just eat perfectly for one day! I would have the plan all laid out in my mind each morning and I would do so well until about four o'clock and then I would blow it every time.

Diets are notorious for setting you up for a perfect 'plan' and then when you blow it they are designed so that it is your entire fault for messing up. No one ever seems to question that the diet could be at fault!

Sometimes I wonder if people can see the battles taking place in my head. I hear thoughts like, 'you can't do that, look at you, you're worthless, who do you think you are?', and I try to rebuttal the thoughts with, 'I'm a child of God, I am worth a lot, and I can do this'. I try and force the negative thoughts down somewhere and it seems almost like it is a physical task to do so. Imagine if our thoughts played out like a movie reel, especially at Sunday morning church services, yikes! (See God is so good to us!)

The deeper I get into God the more and more I begin to understand that I will never be able to live the way I desire for God this side of heaven, because I am encased inside a body and mind that are infiltrated with sin.

Let's take a break from looking within our character and now turn our focus on the character of God. In each of the following passages we will see the character of God emerging but as a side note we will also see a little bit of the character of the evil one, Satan.

In Matthew 13:24-30, Jesus tells a parable:

The kingdom of heaven is like a man who sowed good seed in his field. But while everyone was sleeping, his enemy came and sowed weeds among the wheat, and went away. When the wheat sprouted and formed heads, then the weeds also appeared.

The owner's servants came to him and said, 'Sir didn't you sow good seed in your field? Where then the weeds come from?'

'An enemy did this,' he replied.

'The servants asked him, 'Do you want us to go and pull them up?'

'No,' he answered, 'because while you are pulling the weeds, you may root up the wheat with them. Let both grow together until the harvest. At that time I will tell the harvesters: First collect the weeds and tie them in bundles to be burned; then gather the wheat and bring it into my barn.

Put yourself in the shoes of the farmer; try and think what must have been going through his mind at the time. You have worked hard sowing expensive seed, in fact, you may have just spent everything you and your family had to obtain such good seed. You have done everything you possibly can to ensure that the crop will come up at harvest time. You have prepared the ground, sowed the seed, watered, possible fertilized, checked on it everyday and waited. How do you feel when you see that at harvest time next to every good sprout there is a weed growing, purposefully placed there by someone who does not like you?

Personally, I think the first thing that I would do is probably burst into tears wondering who it was that could do such a thing. After the initial grief, I would move right into anger. I mean I know how expensive it is to buy good seed and you spend all that time preparing the ground and planting the seed, waiting in expectancy for a fantastic crop for months and then only to wake one morning to this!

It's not really about the seed that would upset me but all the time and energy that went into the planting all ruined, wasted. Not to mention the pressure you would be under from your family and workers, probably thinking you didn't get the right stuff in the first place, wasting everyone's time and money. What a situation! What would you do?

When things go really wrong in our lives we tend to do either one of two things. Run like mad in the other direction or work like mad to fix the problem as quickly as we can, before anyone else notices. Both try to create a fresh start or a new beginning. We just want to wipe the board clean and start again, to forget the problem and move on as quickly as possible. The servants here suggest pulling out all of the weeds so the problem no longer exists. But the wise farmer knows that this would create a new problem destroying half of the wheat along with the weeds. No the wise farmer encourages them to just wait and when the time is right, then he will deal with the problem properly.

Imagine if the farmer ran around trying to pull all of the weeds out. He could have run around his field in a frenzy along with all of his workers trying to pull out all of the weeds. He would be doing something, or at least appear to be doing something, to resolve the problem.

However, to accomplish this impossible feat he would have completely exhausted himself and everyone else around him. He would have given himself a heart attack from attempting the physically impossible, plus there was a real danger of pulling out good wheat along with the weeds. He would have destroyed much of the good harvest, doing more harm than good to his field. In the end he would have most likely felt like a failure because he was not able to fix the problem as his heart desired.

Instead he waited. He left it for the appropriate time, the harvest time. This is a skill not many of us have mastered in our fast-paced, demanding society. He thought about the situation and looked past the immediate problem into a long-term solution for his answer. He didn't rush into a fast answer to cover up the problem; he looked for a solution that would actually resolve the problem. He most likely viewed the situation from a variety of angles and in the end waited until the correct answer came to mind.

Now, let's relate this to the weeds in our lives. What weeds are in your life at the moment? A demotion at work, a job you hate, an uncontrollable habit in your life, a person who just never stops tearing you down, an abusive or cheating spouse, a dream that you've given up on, a demolished self esteem, financial loss, or a situation where you feel you have no control?

Whatever they are, I know that they literally break your heart. They are designed by the enemy to do so.

How many of us run around like chickens without their heads trying to pull out every weed as it appears? We are so focused on fixing the problem right now and in our own way that we nearly kill ourselves trying to keeps our lives together.

The weeds in our life are not accidental. They are purposefully placed there by an enemy (not by the farmer). We need to carve this into our brains that God is not out to get us! He created us, loves us. He wants to heal us, free us and give us life to the full. There is no evil in God; he is holy, pure and just. But, there is another force at work here - an enemy.

God doesn't even see our problems as problems! To Him, our problems are just another way for him to teach us and reveal to us more of who he is: all powerful, all knowing, full of grace and mercy. And in His position he will not stoop to our level just to please us. He is holy and unchanging. He was the same yesterday, today and will be the same forever. That should be very comforting as this means he will never trick you or just give up on you and leave you. He will never join forces with your enemies to uproot your happiness and joy in this life. He is on your side!

I emphasize this because I think a big step in working through our problems is taking responsibility for them; another teaching the world has moved away from. Shifting blame does not help anyone; it only isolates you and keeps you from ever solving the problem.

As I related earlier, I once read an e-mailed story about how we can view our problems, and I loved how it ended with this: 'If others cause all my problems, then there is nothing I can do to help. But when I see my own folly and sin; with the Lords strength, I can face it and change. Once I am the cause of my problems; I am also potentially the solution.'

I hope you will understand why when it comes to the difficult problems that run deep into our lives, God will most likely never answer a prayer of: 'Please God, just take (the problem) away'. If he ripped out the problem completely, he may do more damage than good if the time is not right and if He ripped out all of your problems, you would never mature. We need to get our minds around the fact that we can not contain God in our minds. His ways are much higher than ours and we will never be able to understand everything about God. That is why He is God.

Try this exercise. In a moment, I want you to close your eyes and try to envision an apple. Try and feel the texture of it in your mind and the stem sticking out of the top. As you move this apple about in your hand thinking about eating it, I want you to see it clearly. Only the color of this apple is purple. I want you to actually see the purple skin, see even the various shades of purple at the top and bottom of the apple.

As you think about that in one hand, I want you to visualize just as clearly a pink banana in your other hand. Imagine the pink skin as you peel the banana. As you are pondering your fruit you decide to walk outside onto your front lawn. You feel the grass between your toes. As you look at the grass it is a deep velvet red color, similar to the deep red roses you see in garden. Okay, try and visualize!

Truly visualizing these in their different colors is quite difficult. If you are like me you are trying to put the color on top of the fruit but to actually visualize it as a real piece of fruit in that color is another matter.

Now this is a simple exercise but I believe God is trying to get our minds out of the mould they so easily are set in. If you find visualizing fruit in a different color a bit challenging then please realize that when God wants you to see your life from his perspective, He has quite a job cut out for Him and us!

We have grown up with our mind set in a certain way for so long that it is no easy feat to change it. Understanding concepts like, 'God is holy and there is no evil in him', 'God wants the very best for you', and 'you are truly a beautiful person', will take some effort to get your brain around. So open your mind to what God wants to teach you. Don't close off so early just because it doesn't make sense at first.

Let's instead pray for God to show us the 'good wheat' he has sowed. Wheat that is hidden in amongst the weeds. Push down the weeds for a moment and look for what good wheat is there. The quicker we come to understand the good wheat the quicker the time will arrive for harvest.

Take a moment now and try and think of what good wheat you may find in the midst of the problems that break your heart.

Jesus explains this parable further in Matthew 13:36-43:

The one who sowed the good seed is the Son of Man. The field is the world, and the good seed stands for the sons of the kingdom. The weeds are the sons of the evil one, and the enemy who sows them is the devil. The harvest is the end of the age, and the harvesters are the angels.

As the weeds are pulled up and burned in the fire, so it will be at the end of the age. The Son of Man will send out his angels, and they will weed out of his kingdom everything that causes sin and all who do evil. They will throw them into the fiery furnace, where there will be weeping and gnashing of teeth. Then the righteous will shine like the sun in the kingdom of their Father. He who has ears, let him hear.

We are spiritual beings and we are living in a spiritual world, whether you like it or not. You can pretend that none of this exists or you can line yourself up with God and let him teach you how to live in such a way that the enemy can no longer have hold over you.

The good news is that if we look closely at the end of this passage, there will be a time when God does take away the problem! Timing is crucial, yet time in itself is so irrelevant to God. All things are possible for him so he is not worried and neither should you be.

Have a look at another parable found in Luke 8:5-8:

A farmer went out to sow his seed. As he was scattering the seed, some fell along the path; it was trampled on. And the birds of the air ate it up.

Some fell on rock, and when it came up, the plants withered because they had no moisture.

Other seed fell among thorns, which grew up with it and choked the plants.

Still other seed fell on good soil. It came up and yielded a crop, a hundred times more than was sown.

This parable is further explained in Luke 8:11-15:

The seed is the word of God. Those along the path are the ones who hear, and then the devil comes and takes away the word from their hearts, so that they may not believe and be saved.

Those on the rock are the ones who receive the word with joy when they hear it, but they have no root. They believe for a while, but in the time of testing they fall away.

The seed that fell among thorns stand for those who hear, but as they go on their way they are choked by life's worries, riches and pleasures, and they do not mature.

But the seed on good soil stands for those with a noble and good heart, who hear the word, retain it, and by persevering produce a crop.

When you feel like God is telling you something, how do you respond? Do you think about it for a moment then push it aside with all the other thoughts of a busy day? Do you want to do something about it but just never get around to it? Do you genuinely try to act on it but the pressure of family and friends or the ways of the world make you give up? Or do you take what you feel is being said and spend time praying about it, reading about it, talking about it then acting upon it?

As soon as you grasp the meaning of a God-given lesson, the enemy will do everything possible to strip that away from you. Some of the most heated family arguments will occur before or after a powerful church service. Times of depression, loneliness, discontentment, anger and complacency will most often occur before or after a great thing of God. The most classic examples are stories told in the Bible of David, Elijah, Samson and Peter.

I can pretty much tell if what I am doing is of God or not, just by looking at the struggles of those who try attempting godly things with me. I think back on all the things that I have had the privilege to be involved with, dealing with great and powerful acts of God and I can't recall once not having opposition. It comes in all forms. Some you can recognize as attacks but others you are too far into it to realize you are having the wool pulled over your eyes.

We want to make sure that we allow God's word to take root so that it may flourish and grow in our lives and we may live in the freedom he desires us to have. These are the things that allow God's word to grow: praying, obeying immediately, serving Him with your whole heart, seeking guidance from others who walk in the ways of God, trusting God, having faith in God, reading the Bible in fact memorizing it, if you can.

I think memorizing truths of the Bible is so excellent because you always have it with you no matter what the circumstance. You can't always have the Bible on hand and you may not be hearing from God at the current time but by storing his word away in your mind and heart, you can cling onto the word until you do hear from God.

In John 10:1-18 Jesus distinguishes between himself and those associated with the evil one. Verses 7 to 13 say:

I tell you the truth. I am the gate for the sheep. All who ever came before me were thieves and robbers, but the sheep did not listen to them. I am the gate; whoever enters through me will be saved. He will come in and go out, and find pasture. The thief comes only to steal and kill and destroy; I have come that they may have life, and have it to the full.

I am the good shepherd. The good shepherd lays down his life for the sheep. The hired hand is not the shepherd who owns the sheep. So when he sees the wolf coming, he abandons the sheep and runs away. Then the wolf attacks the flock and scatters it. The man runs away because he is a hired hand and cares nothing for the sheep.

The good shepherd is open and honest, entering the sheep pen by the gate, where the thief and robber deceive the sheep by climbing in by other ways. The shepherd calls his sheep by name and knows them intimately. He goes ahead of them to protect them and never leaves them.

The shepherd is the only way: there are a lot of well-meaning hired hands who may try and help you with their wisdom but when the struggles come, they are long gone while the shepherd remains. He is around long after the wolf-frightened hired hand has run away. He lays his life down for his sheep so that they may live, not just living to exist but to have life and have it to the full.

I will make short mention here of the enemy, not that he deserves any mention but I think it is worth knowing what we are dealing with. I recommend that you read Revelation 12, keeping in mind that this is a spiritual view of the enemy.

The devil is not a fictional, red-colored character with horns on his head. He is very real and within him lays everything that I hate; rape, murder, lies, gossip, deceit, hurt, entrapment, bondage, cultic activity and death. He is not out to just put a stumbling block in your way, he is out to totally destroy you. He wants you to die with him. Evil always wants company and the devil is no exception.

1 Peter 5:8 states:

Be self-controlled and alert. Your enemy the devil prowls around like a roaring lion looking for someone to devour.

How does the lion roar in your life? Often we feel the lion is stalking us, trying to make us fearful of things. His presence seems to unnerve us. Several times the lion pounces upon us, taking us unexpectedly into areas we prefer not to travel. But to hear the lion roar is an experience that one never seems to forget. He roars so close to your face that you can feel the warmth of his breath. The roar is so loud, so deafening that you can't seem to hear anything else. Your whole body senses danger and it feels as if you have nowhere to go. You are caught and about to be devoured.

I heard nothing else but this roar as I came to the end of my journey with an eating disorder. I remember thinking: 'I just can't take this any more!' It was a very close brush with death. I just wanted anything to get me out of the vicious cycle that I was in. I could not go on living life in the same way any more.

Now, you may have never experienced a real lion, the furry kind, attacking you but the Bible tells us that there is a very real spiritual lion hunting you. And when the lion roars, it is the time in your life where you have reached the end of your rope. All hope is gone. You feel completely alone. Everything is dark and you wonder why you were brought into this world in the first place.

Friends try to offer encouragement but the roar is so load that you can't hear their words any more. You feel trapped and there doesn't seem to be a way out. Prayers seem to be hitting the ceiling and you begin to wonder if there is a God or, if there is, how could he be so cruel? The questions and doubts flood your brain.

How can you escape? Let's read on (1 Peter 5: 9-11),

Resist him, standing firm in the faith, because you know that the family of believers throughout the world is undergoing the same kind of sufferings.

And the God of all grace, who called you to his eternal glory in Christ, after you have suffered a little while, will himself restore you and make you strong, firm and steadfast. To him be the power for ever and ever. Amen

Resist him Don't give in but give up. What I mean is give it up to God. Choose God. Leave all feeling, emotion and rationalization out of it. Simply choose God.

Standing firm in the faith This is the only thing you have to 'do', stand and believe in God, that he is who he says and that he will come through for you.

Because you know that your brothers throughout the world are undergoing the same kind of suffering You are not alone. There is not a problem that exists in your life that has not been suffered by someone else. There is support for you and eventually, you will be a support for others.

And the God of all grace By the way, God does own all grace. The little we have is a gift from him and is not of ourselves.

Who called you to his eternal glory in Christ He who has called you has not left you, or lost you, or forgotten you. This is especially true during times of hardship and suffering.

After you have suffered a little while He has never promised a life without suffering, in fact, I challenge you to find one person in the Bible that did not suffer. The good news is there is a time limit to your suffering. Jesus promises a day when he will take all suffering away.

Will himself restore you and make you strong, firm and steadfast Now that is a promise! He doesn't just restore you back to where you were. He adds to this strength, steadiness, and firmness to make you better than you were before.

To him be the power for ever and ever. Amen. He will do it for His own glory, not because you beg and plead but because it is his nature to love you, heal you and make you better for it.

When God does deliver you, I do pray that you give him the glory and learn the lessons he has taught you or you may find yourself back in a similar situation. I don't know about you but I try and learn God's lessons as quickly as possible so that I will not have to relearn the lesson in another painful situation.

I recognize that there are always questions that will try to fill your mind with doubt but the more I learn of God and His character the more I begin to understand He has provided the way, if we will just line ourselves up with his ways.

On a broad scale thoughts may plague us about the world around us. For example, why does God allow so many people to starve in the world?

There will never be a simple answer for life's questions because God is so complex but we can see enough to give God the benefit of the doubt. If you look closely at this problem God has given ample amounts of food to feed the world over several times. The problem lies in the human factor; the distribution of the goods and basically greed verses loving each other.

On a more individual scale, we may wonder why God allows us to go through so many problems and heartaches in our life if He loves us so much. Again the answer is never an easy one but I do know God never wastes an opportunity to teach us through these struggles. He allows us the choice to go our way or his. It's always easier to blame God then to face the reality of our own sinfulness and to take accountability for our own actions. When you honestly look at what we do when we are in control, we stuff it up every time. Let's return to Him and allow Him to help us be the great people He designed us to be.

Notes:

82

Chapter Six
Accountability

I'll never forget watching a Christmas pageant at church one year. The children were humbly costumed to their parts. It was not a huge church and one could tell the budget was minimal for such productions!

Anyways, after baby Jesus had arrived at Mary and Joseph's side, the angels came out to proclaim the good news. They were all dressed in white bed sheets with some gold piping over their heads shaped into halos. The angels came in all sizes. The largest one, who was about 12 years old, happened to stand in front of where I was sitting. An elderly gentleman sitting next to me said in what he thought was a quiet whisper, 'looks more like a white elephant'.

If there is one thing that raises my anger very quickly it is fat jokes or comments on people's weight or appearance. I know I am a biased with my background here but I just don't understand why people feel they have to share their thoughts aloud to others. Do they think that an overweight person doesn't know they are big or that their comments will suddenly make the person think, 'Hey, you're right! I'm gonna go on a diet and change that!' The only thing comments like that will do to a person is lower his or her self-esteem or demolish it all together.

It seems that every man or woman struggling with weight or self-esteem issues has had and continues to have several people surrounding them armed with a plethora of judgmental comments under their belt. If it's not in the comment, it is in the look or the not-so-subtle hints of Jenny Craig or Weight Watchers pamphlets placed inconspicuously around the house or office. Yes, we are surrounded by media which hounds in the point that thin, buff and beautiful is the only way to go but at least we can turn off the TV or not buy the magazines, but how do you 'turn off' or 'mute' the people that you live and work with?

Although there are always going to people around us with opinionated judgements and downright rude and hurtful comments, judging others by their weight or looks is wrong. The Bible is very clear on this issue. In fact, even God does not judge by external appearances. Here are just a few of the many passages found in the Bible on this subject:

Do not judge, or you too will be judged. For in the same way you judge others, you will be judged, and with the measure you use, it will be measured to you.

Matthew 7:1-2

As for those who seemed to be important - whatever they were makes no difference to me; God does not judge by external appearance...

Galatians 2:6

Accept him whose faith is weak, without passing judgment on disputable matters. One man's faith allows him to eat everything, but another man, whose faith is weak, eats only vegetables. The man who eats everything must not look down on him who does not, and the man who does not eat everything must not condemn the man who does, for God has accepted him. Who are you to judge someone else's servant? To his own master he stands or falls. And he will stand, for the Lord is able to make him stand.

Romans 14:1-4

What keeps me calm when people say such cruel things is the gentle reminder from God that I'm not perfect either. Many times I have also failed to look beyond the appearances of various people.

I too can have a judgmental attitude. This is why we are going to look first at ourselves before we consider those around us. In areas of conflict, I believe this is the godly order of looking at things: God first, ourselves next and then finally how to resolve situations with those around us.

Why do you look at the speck of sawdust in your brother's eye and pay no attention to the plank in your own eye? How can you say to your brother, 'let me take the speck out of your eye' when all the time there is a plank in your own eye? You hypocrite, first take the plank out of your own eye, and then you will see clearly to remove the speck from your brother's eye.

Matthew 7:3-5

As we have seen in the previous verses, a judgmental heart is wrong yet so is revenge and unrighteous anger. We have got to get our minds in the right state before we attempt to confront people, otherwise we could possibly make the situation even worse than it already is.

Put on the full armor of God so that you can take your stand ...

Stand firm then, with the belt of truth buckled around your waist, with the breastplate of righteousness in place, and with your feet fitted with the readiness that comes from the gospel of peace. In addition to all this, take up the shield of faith, with which you can extinguish all the flaming arrows of the evil one. Take the helmet of salvation and the sword of the Spirit, which is the word of God. And pray in the Spirit on all occasions with all kinds of prayers and requests. With this in mind, be alert and always keep on praying for all the saints.

Ephesians 6:10-18

Athletes go into training before they compete. A soldier must put on armor before he goes into a battle. If care is not taken in the time of preparation neither will have much of a chance to make the distance or in the case of a soldier to make it out alive.

When you take up the armor of God, you are able to stand and stand firm. God knows the biggest battles you will ever fight are in your mind, so his armor includes items of a spiritual nature. Notice the first piece of armor that is mentioned is the belt of truth.

If you can't face the truth about yourself or speak in truth to others, you will not be able to get very far in the battles of life. Jesus says, 'I am the way, truth and the life.' (John 14:6). If you want to go His way, you have to operate in the truth so that you may find life. Once you are able to move in truth the other pieces of armor come from spending time with God.

I need to give an example here so you can really see the battle taking place while you are not in the heat of it. I think we all can relate to the fact that once you are in the thick of a battle with words, it's too late to think rationally.

Let's say that you are having dinner at a close relative's place. The whole family has been invited and there are around 15 people in the room. You have finished dinner and the host is about to serve dessert. You are pleasantly surprised how well the evening has been because in years past at every family event someone always manages to make a comment about your weight.

The dessert is a beautiful homemade chocolate mud cake. As the host begins to cut the cake into pieces you notice that your piece is just about a quarter of the size of everyone else's. She begins to hand out the plates of cake to everyone seated around the table yet when she comes to you she says, 'I also have fruit salad if you'd rather have that instead.'

You reply: 'Why? I'm not on a diet or anything.'

There is an uncomfortable silence and the host then proceeds to say: 'Oh, I just assumed you were trying to lose some excess weight before summer begins. You used to be the prettiest girl in our town. It's been years now since you've had the kids and you know what they say, 'if you don't get the weight off soon, you will be stuck with it forever.''

As you look up, everyone is nodding their head in agreement and begin talking about all the methods they have used to lose weight fast.

Now I want you to truthfully detail exactly how you would respond.

I have been in hundreds of situations like this and the emotional level doesn't get any higher than at these particular times. Responses are numerous and can include a range from absolute silence to bursting into tears and running out of the room to getting verbally or even physically abusive. None of which I would classify under a Godly response. These are natural responses of the human nature but God wants so much more for us.

When we are in the human state of mind we inevitably lose control and rarely end up with the desired outcome. If you are a Christian, this is so crucial because your response is what people will attribute to Christianity in general. Christian or not, you potentially can ruin how people view you forever. It is very hard to go back and change these historical moments.

The following is not easy yet is very possible with God's strength. It requires a major change in the way you think and feel. But when you finally get your mind around this it will change you and many other people around you, including the family and friends you deem unchangeable.

First, I want you to take a good, hard look at yourself. Do you view others according to their appearance? I am not just talking about weight issues here. I want you to scroll through the many people you encounter in your everyday life and think about how you treat them.

What about new people that you meet? Have you formed an opinion of them within the first 15 minutes of meeting them?

You can forgive someone and still maintain your personal boundaries.

How do you view others who have disabilities, come from other countries with different beliefs than you hold, have contrary opinions and ideas to you?

Do you give the boss or the cleaning lady the same opportunity to know you as your work colleagues? Or does the basis of your friendships require they be similar to you?

Does age pose a barrier to friendships? Do children? How about a person living in 'sin'?
How do you view a person who has had a past full of mistakes?

How about someone who has hurt or offended you before? Can you come to understand that all of us are in a process of growing, maturing and changing? The person who offended you days ago may not be the same person today. Are you giving them the opportunity to change?

Notice that I am not saying that tolerance is the go here. Our society has made a real mess out of that one. What I am saying is that forgiveness and trust are two different things. You can forgive someone and still maintain your personal boundaries. Do you hold forgiveness and grace before others or are you just as guilty of judging as the people who are judging you?

88

I would encourage you to take some time to ponder the people whom Jesus deemed as valuable enough to spend some time getting to know and opening himself up to. Jesus spent time with sinners, taught sinners, loved sinners yet did not in any way condone sin. He forgave those who hurt or offended him so they could discover another way of living; with peace and inner stillness unlike anything exemplified in this world. He set an example so others could see they had the capacity to live like this too.

When people see good being lived out by others they are moved to be better people themselves. This is why Jesus says to pray for your enemies. If their hearts are softened and their minds are opened then they may begin to understand and change. And if you think God has done miracles with your life, just wait to see what He can do with theirs.

What criteria do you place on yourself to be what is in your mind 'acceptable'?

Do you place the same criteria of acceptance on others? Why, or why not?

When it does come to physical appearance, are you guilty of the very offense you are holding others accountable for? What things arouse anger or envy about the way others are eating around you? Are you jealous of those who have conquered their weight problem or of those who have never struggled with weight issues?

I will never forget a question posed at a church service I attended while in college. The pastor asked if there was anyone in the room who was perfectly happy with the way they looked. Only one hand went up in the room and it was a fellow student sitting two rows in front of me.

Initially I was shocked that anyone could feel this way. Then I immediately went to work looking for all of the flaws I could find on this poor girl. Within seconds I moved right into anger, thinking to myself: 'What a snob! She must be so in love with herself she doesn't even notice the people around her struggling to be so perfect!' From anger, I moved into jealousy. Talk about an emotional roller coaster. I don't even remember what the sermon was about because I was so immersed in this girl and her response to a simple question.

Now that I am perfectly happy with the way I look, I feel sad about that experience from the past. Nearly every hand should have gone up in the room that day. We can be happy with the way we look. It is a skill we need to learn before we begin working on changing anything about our appearance. If you don't learn the skill of being content in all situations then you will never find contentment. Some examples of this in the realm of self-image range from anorexia to the latest trend of extreme makeovers involving high-risk cosmetic surgery, where people just never seem satisfied and keep taking things further and further.

Take some real time out to examine yourself with brutal honesty. Next state what you have done wrong out loud, with no one around but you and God. Bring them out to view openly before God. Can you come to grips with the fact that you are not perfect? All of us have sides to us that we do not like and sides to us that other people do not like. The only thing that changes that is a soft heart and a teachable mind and the power of God.

We need to understand that people have very different mindsets. Right or wrong we have to acknowledge these differences.

One man considers one day more sacred than another; another man considers everyday alike. Each one should be fully convinced in his own mind. He who regards one day as special, does so to the

Lord. He who eats meat, eats to the Lord, for he gives thanks to God; and he who abstains, does so to the Lord and gives thanks to God.

For none of us lives to himself alone and none of us dies to himself alone. If we live, we live to the Lord; and if we die, we die to the Lord. So, whether we live or die, we belong to the Lord. For this very reason, Christ died and returned to life so that he might be the Lord of both the dead and the living.

Romans 14:5-9

People have different ways of thinking. We have been influenced by our family, our education, our culture and our experiences, This is good because if we all thought the same, no one would ever change, discover new ideas or grow. As we mature, we can listen to varying opinions and choose those that work for us and set aside those that are of no value to us. Sometimes people need to agree to disagree. The best result is obtained by continuing a healthy relationship through disagreements.

As a teacher I can tell you that it is very frustrating when you are trying to get a point across and your students don't get it (and honestly there are many times they just don't want to get it). They are happy the way they are. Should I get offended by a student just because he doesn't grasp the idea or even care? No, an educator is expected to be bigger than that. It would be ridiculous to be offended every time a student disagreed or voiced his lack of interest. So what can you do? You move on and continue going, giving that student the same respect and treatment that you do everyone else and pray that one day it will sink in and the attitude will change.

There are many more occasions where I as a teacher need to realize that I am only teaching one of many different ways to achieve a desired outcome and a student may choose to try a different method. They may be convinced that their method is the only correct way of going about it. As long as we end up with a desired outcome, I need to allow them the freedom of doing it their way.

Like the miniature society of a classroom, so it is with many folks around us. Many don't have a weight problem nor have any understanding of what you are going through or how you feel. Others are fully convinced that their method of losing weight is the only way. In their minds they believe that if you just stick to the program, it should work for you too. Some honestly just don't care and it is very frustrating indeed. No matter what others think or do around us, it does not give us permission to lose control and act in ways that we know are not right just because we are angry or offended. Neither do we have to simply agree with other people.

Being forever silent is not the answer either because it gives the impression that what they are doing is okay. The only time I would endorse silence is when you are not in control of yourself. Then I would encourage you to silently move away from the person until you regain your composure and then go back to confront the issue. (Notice here that I say confront the issue, not attack the person.)

Now, let's return to the example above. How should we have responded? Before you do anything at all, it might be a good idea to discern what motive lay behind the comments that upset you. Is this really a weight issue? Or is there something else that needs to be mended in your relationship?

Are these words and actions retaliation for something you have done to hurt this person in the past? Do think this person is feeling threatened by you or others around you? Take a moment to put yourself in other person's shoes. Are there some issues in this person's life that cause them to act the way they do? Do you care? Really?

When we begin to think of others first we strengthen our own self-confidence. Please think about that statement carefully. When you are so absorbed in yourself and your feelings all the time, comments tend to sting even more. Before you know it you begin to take every comment the wrong way. When you take the focus off of yourself and examine what is happening in the lives of those around you, you become strong. You are no longer depending on others to determine your self-worth but are encouraging others and therefore strengthening both of you in self-confidence.

By thinking through these issues first you begin to allow some of the steam to be released from the pressure cooker before any response is made at all.

The Bible says,

'Therefore, I urge you, brothers in view of God's mercy, to offer your bodies as living sacrifices, holy and pleasing to God-this is your spiritual act of worship. Do not conform any longer to the pattern of this world, but be transformed by the renewing of your mind.'

Romans 12:1-2

After you have thought these things through and are experiencing the fruit of the spirit, namely self-control, then I urge you to take action. The first thing is to get the host away from the rest of the party. This may mean to remain silent until you are able to confront the person one on one. I suggest this because it is not a show and confronting someone in front of others will only put them on the defensive. The guards will be up as they don't want to look bad in front of anyone else. Just because they have done it to you, does not mean that you have to stoop to their level of disrespect.

After you get them away from the situation you need to speak to them in a loving and firm way. Gather your thoughts before you speak and don't let them distract you from dealing with the issue. I would encourage you to speak briefly about the issue, go into how it made you feel and then, if necessary, set a boundary.

For example, I would say something like: 'When you suggested that I needed to be on a diet in front of the whole family, I felt very hurt and embarrassed. This is an area that is very sensitive to me and when and if I am ready to talk about it with you, I will call you. Until then I would prefer that this area not be brought up again.'

You may find that simply confronting the person on the issue may be enough for things to change. It may simply open the door for conversation about this area or may offer opportunity to mend any previous damage in your relationship. However, if you feel that what you said was not heard and you are not getting anywhere, you may then need to set a boundary. 'If you feel you need to make hurtful comments about me again, I will leave the room.' You will have to find a boundary that you are happy with, remembering the goal is to restore relationships.

Unfortunately, if reoccurrences of the incident occur it may be necessary to set strong boundaries until you feel you can cope. For example, 'I am not comfortable eating dinner at your house as you insist on discussing my weight every time I am in your presence. If you continue making me feel this way, I will not come to your house for a meal.'

Just remember, how you speak is just as important as what you say. Combative and threatening boundaries are not helpful. Boundaries that are clear yet allow room for the improvement of your relationship are the best boundaries to set. Set boundaries with the goal of reconciliation in mind. The goal is to improve the relationship not destroy it.

I would try to end the conversation with what you would desire as the end outcome. 'Look, I really want to have a better relationship with you and I hope you understand that while I really desire this relationship I will not accept abusive treatment from you anymore.' These responses take time, planning and self-control. We tend to replay the negative scenes in our minds so often. Let's start replaying those scenes with the possible positive endings.

Even with the best devised plans and self-control made of steel, you need to prepare yourself because nine times out of ten you will not get the desired response or even any attempt on their behalf to mend the situation. However, I can not stress enough it is still important that you do what is right.

It is written: 'As surely as I live,' says the Lord, 'every knee will bow before me; every tongue will confess to God.' So then, each of us will give an account of himself to God. Therefore let us stop passing judgment on one another. Instead, make up your mind not to put any stumbling block or obstacle in your brother's way.

Romans 14:11-13

Watch what comes out of your mouth yet be bold enough to speak up to and for others. By sticking to your resolve to do what is right, you will do several things. First and most importantly, you will please God. One day each of us will give an account for how we lived this life, what we have said and done to the children of God around us. Secondly, you will learn so much about yourself and begin to realize that you are the only one that allows other people's comments to affect you. Finally, over time you will begin to change the way people think and speak around you.

It is a good idea to start small and work your way up to confronting the people who you really don't want to confront. Start with friends who are already on your side and tell them you are practicing confronting people with love and grace. If you are married, you really need to communicate to your spouse what you are going through and enlist his or her help.

I will never forget the first time I went on a long trip with my soon to be husband. I had never discussed nor was I planning on ever discussing my eating disorder with anyone. We had been in the car for several hours and had stopped at a service station to fill the car with petrol. I told Mark that I needed to go to the toilet and that I would meet him back at the car in a few minutes.

On the way to the toilet, I bought two chocolate bars. I went to the toilet and snuck back to the car with the chocolate hidden in my purse. Mark had just finished filling the tank and said he needed to go to the toilet as well. While he was away, I ripped open the chocolate and started to shovel it in. I had just finished off the last piece and had a smug smile on my face that I had gotten away with it, when he did the unimaginable. Instead of just getting back into the car to drive, much to my horror and dismay, he came to my side of the car to give me a kiss!

Well, as you can imagine it didn't take long before he noticed that I had eaten chocolate. Mark pulled back and said: 'Did you just eat chocolate?' I didn't know what to do or say as memories of the many negative comments from the past came flooding in. He continued: 'Why didn't you get me one?' Then he turned around and walked back to buy his own. I cannot explain to you what happened in me that day. It was the first time I felt completely loved and accepted for who I was and it began a new hope in me that I didn't want to ever stop.

After we were married, I told him about my eating disorder and what that day meant to me. As the communication line was open I was able to speak openly and frankly about the eating problem that I had struggled with for so long. He wanted to know what he could do to help so I decided to continue on the line of being frank and honest and told him specifically what I needed.

When I ordered a meal at a restaurant, I needed to feel free to eat whatever I wanted without any criticism. When I pulled out ice cream or chocolate at home I wanted to be able to eat it out in the open without any funny looks or negative comments. In fact, it would be nice if occasionally he joined me. When I asked him how I looked, I needed him to say beautiful and look like he really meant it. I asked him to never mention dieting or anything related to it ever again. If others said anything to me about my weight, I needed him to stick up for me.

As he so lovingly met these requests I no longer felt I had to hide anything from him. Our relationship grew as I knew he would back me up no matter what the situation. It developed a deep love. As things were brought into the open and I no longer had to face condemnation, I no longer felt the need to hide and slowly no longer felt the need to eat the things I didn't want to eat in the first place.

> When I ordered a meal at a restaurant, I needed to feel free to eat whatever I wanted without any criticism.

No man lives to himself alone, why then do we try to overcome our problems alone. If you are married you need to take the time to discuss what help you need from your spouse and be specific! If you are single then enlist your best friend or a sibling to help you out.

Once we begin changing our mindsets to take on God's mindset and begin to communicate with others in a Godly manner then we are ready to make some changes. If we are encouraging others around us to change then we need to be willing to go there ourselves. We need to start looking at old and ugly habits and replace them with new. The most significant way is by changing what comes out of our mouths.

I remember once going to a beautiful buffet lunch put on just for the ladies of our church. As I began to dish out a bit of everything on the table, the woman in front of me said, 'a moment on the lips, forever on the hips', and the woman behind me said, 'that one will be worth 15 points!' Several ladies behind her giggled and nodded in agreement. Another woman at the dessert table said, 'Oh, this is absolutely wicked!'

Although the comments were directed to the food and not me, it didn't make me feel any better. I began to look at my plate of food and what looked so beautiful before suddenly had a cloudy overcast upon it. I couldn't decide if I felt guilty for what I was going to enjoy or depressed that no one else was enjoying it. My eyes were drawn to the caterer, and although the comments were in no way directed to the caterer of the buffet, I began to notice a change in her demeanor as she stood listening to the comments. She looked disappointed. Why do we do this to ourselves and others around us?

As one who is in the Lord, Jesus, I am fully convinced that no food is unclean in itself.   *Romans 14:14*

Paul is speaking in reference to specific foods that were offered to idols. There is no food that is spiritually 'off-limits' by God's standards. (See also Acts 10:9-23). So if food is not sinful, what is? Food is neither wicked nor sinful. It is what we do with food that becomes sinful. For example, do we use it as a comfort source instead of God? It is also what we say and do to each other on account of food that is sinful. Judging, criticizing and condemning ourselves and others destroys everything that Jesus stood for and died for. Do the words we speak show love, joy, peace, patience, kindness, goodness, gentleness and self-control; the very characteristics of the Holy Spirit. (Galatians 5:22-23)

So whatever you believe about these things keep between yourself and God. Blessed is the man who does not condemn himself by what he approves. But the man who has doubts is condemned if he eats, because his eating is not from faith; and everything that does not come from faith is sin.   Romans 14:22

Do you ever find yourself saying similar things like, 'you'll pay for that tomorrow', 'a moment on the lips' or 'you are what you eat'? I want to encourage you to start a new type of talk with a language that doesn't just follow a trend of what everyone else is saying. We not only need to change the way we speak for ourselves but for those who are looking on.

The rate of younger and younger girls dieting is just alarming. Eating disorders and abnormal dieting is now becoming a problem in the early years of primary schools. Girls who shouldn't even know they have a self-image are struggling with the way they look. They feel they need to look like the older girls they see on Facebook or on television. They are constantly checking Instagram, Facebook and Messaging to see what their friends are posting. They have the skill of taking 'Selfies' down to an art.

Mothers, older sisters and close friends can have a greater influence now than ever. Young girls are watching the women of our generation to learn what should be important in life. What are we doing to our younger sisters? I want to start teaching the young girls and women around me that there is so much more to life than the way we eat or look.

Let's stop the vicious cycle of condemning comments and start a cycle of uplifting and encouraging comments. The best person to start this cycle is you. When others begin to see how good you make them feel, and the many friends surrounding you, they will want to follow your lead. When we give compliments to people around us, let's start appreciating people for who they are instead of continuing in the world's focus on appearance. No wonder people have a hard time accepting compliments when they are only focused on the surface level of who we are.

We say, 'Oh, that's a nice outfit' or 'I love your hair' focusing on the surface appearance. Can we start to notice others and appreciate the things they do and say that move us to be better people? For example: 'I saw the way you kept your cool when that woman was tearing you to shreds. You really inspire me to work on controlling my temper.' Or: 'I've noticed your commitment to the kid's program at church and I just want to thank you; it means a lot to me and my family.' Or even, 'you know, you are a beautiful woman inside and out. Your words are always full of grace.' It's impossible to fake a comment when you are looking at someone's character. A comment like that will keep going long after the outfit has dated and the color has come out of the hair!

Begin to look for ways to live your life better and for opportunities to make a positive difference. Take what would normally be stressful events for women and work to make them times of encouragement and uplifting. For example, let's change the way we do Christmas each year.

I use this example because of what Christmas means to dieters. Christmas is the one time of year our focus should be on encouraging and loving each other, sharing in the joy of the season, yet among dieters it is the most dreaded occasion of each year. Even though Christmas is just once a year, the effects last the whole year long. People are dieting, worrying and fretting for what is to come or trying to cope with all the comments and wounds that occurred last year during the actual day of battle.

Many dieters starve themselves for weeks before Christmas so that they can gorge themselves on all the food surrounding the holiday events. They worry about how they will get through the season without putting on an additional amount of weight. Most dread going to family functions for fear of the disapproving looks and rude comments about their weight. They worry and fret what family members will say this year that will sink them lower into a pit of depression.

I think Christmas is the best example of the spiritual battle that we are in. It is supposed to be a season of remembering all the Lord has done for us yet the world (with the devil's help) has managed to turn it into one of the biggest self-centered, greedy, money-making, emotionally and physically draining times of the year. Maybe it should just be called 'mas' (Spanish for 'more') because without Christ you just end up with more heartache, more stress and more junk. Christmas should be a time to focus on the real meaning of life. Unfortunately, most people don't realize that this is only found in the power and glory of the Lord Jesus Christ.

Even when we are in the middle of the year, I hear women fretting and worrying about the Christmas season ahead. A close friend of mine was recently telling me about how she was absolutely dreading the Christmas season this year.

'Every year I dread going to Christmas dinner with my family. All they do is make fun of how I look. They still call me names from my childhood. Nothing I ever do is right for them. It's like they all enjoy coming together so they can have fun putting me down. I wish I could just stay home and have Christmas with my children'.

When I asked her why she continued to go each year, she said she felt she had to go. It was expected of her.

Do you find yourself in a similar predicament each year? I pray not, but if you do, I want to encourage you to do what is in your heart. If you would rather stay home with your immediate family, then do so. Your spouse and children would probably be relieved to get their mother back again instead of a stressed-out, psycho woman they see every other Christmas. Forcing yourself to go places that you don't want to be is really no fun for anyone, especially for you.

If you don't want to see the extended family all in one day, then don't. Explain to them that your family needs to be at home this year alone for special bonding time. Why not schedule to see particular family members for an hour or two on the days surrounding Christmas? That way they won't be able to gang up on you and you will most likely find there will be quality time to share with various family members. You may even want to explain to them that Christmas is just so frantic and stressful that you would prefer to see them separately this year. Who knows, maybe you will start some new traditions.

I find there are similar anxieties about Christmas dinner. People feel they have to eat everything or they will offend someone. Then everyone sits around in somewhat of a comatose state just staring at each other. The 'regret' talk begins. 'Oh, I ate too much!', 'I won't need to eat for weeks', 'Guess I'll have to make some New Years' resolutions to lose weight', etc. Some just nod off to sleep while others feel bloated and sick. No wonder people get so anxious over the whole event.

Let's start a new cycle of events. Instead of gorging out on food, why not eat normal portions and freeze the rest for the weeks to come? Give the extra food away to a backpacker's lodge or a homeless shelter. Instead of just sitting around after eating, play some games, go for a walk together, sing and dance and put on a Christmas show for each other. Even if no one else wants to join in, take yourself off for a nice peaceful walk after eating. Offer to walk the dog.

By making changes to the way we live and view life, others around us will notice there is a better way. We no longer need to conform to old and ugly habits but can experience refreshing life changes.

For the kingdom of God is not a matter of eating and drinking but of righteousness, peace and joy in the Holy Spirit, because anyone who serves Christ in this way is pleasing to God and approved by men. Let us therefore make every effort to do what leads to peace and to mutual edification. Do not destroy the work of God for the sake of food.   Romans 14:17-20

The key to overcoming is being well prepared beforehand so you are not caught off guard. Take the time to get creative with the solutions to your problems when you are not in the middle of the fighting ground. Develop a plan with God and stick to it. Depend on God and He will get you through the toughest of times.

No temptation has seized you except what is common to man. And God is faithful; he will not let you be tempted beyond what you can bear. But when you are tempted, he will also provide a way out so that you can stand up under it.   1 Corinthians 10:13

Notes:

Chapter Seven
The Plan

O kay, now we are getting into what most people are waiting for, the plan. I always loved having a plan as it gave me a sense of hope of finding my way out of the mess I was currently in; similar to a map. However, this plan may be quite different to any other plan you have experienced before. We have to get used to the fact that God will never do things in the exact way that we expect Him to. But that's great news! It means we can expect something different than the last diets we have tried.

Every time I tell people about this program, I always get one of two responses. Either the person tries to guess any dieting tips I supposably teach or they desperately want to know what plan there is to follow. They basically just want to skip straight to 'the plan'. However, you cannot fast track the things of God. If we have a predetermined mindset before coming to God for answers, we will not hear properly and may miss out on all of the good things God has in store for us. Even when God reveals His plans to us, they take time to understand and apply, as we are attempting to change what lies in the very core of our being.

I find that each time God offers a plan for his people to follow, the words are quite simple yet the concepts take many hours of meditation, listening for God's particular way to apply it to our personal lives. Look at the plan of salvation. Simple so that even the most simple people can understand it yet so deep that it takes the rest of your life to live it out and begin to really understand it. Take for example another 'simple' list for living from God, the Ten Commandments. I mean there are only ten of them to follow, how hard could it be? Yet when Jesus expounds on these commands in the New Testament, we catch a glimpse of how in depth they really are.

When I was in prayer about what God had in mind for me to teach specifically for dieters, he gave me the following passages and said: 'Psalm 16 is my diet plan and Psalm 32 is how to follow it.' As simple as they are, it has taken months for me to really start understanding the principles that lay behind these words of wisdom. I will break down each psalm to explain the revelation that I have received from God about each passage. However, once I begin to open the door of understanding it is really up to you to take these passages before God and find out what they mean for your life.

So let's get into it. Psalm 16

Verses 1&2: Keep me safe, O God, for in you I take refuge. I said to the Lord, 'You are my Lord; apart from you I have no good thing.'

When things just get to be 'too much' and you are not having a very good day, what do you do to comfort yourself?

My two 'comfort' places that I would run to would be a book or the television, both washed down with my favorite junk food of the day. I attempted to achieve a comatose state of mind where I would try and drown myself in sheer pleasure. It was as if everything just got to be too hard and this was my little island of escape. The only problem being that every high has a low and at the end of every fantasy awaits reality.

When I was finished trying to forget, everything would come flooding back with a vengeance. The battle in my mind began. 'What was I thinking? Oh, I feel sick. Oh no, I must have just put on 10 pounds just in junk food alone! Now what am I going to do?

I'll never be able to lose this weight! Why can't I control myself?' On and on the thoughts would just keep rolling in. To try and escape this pit of despair, I would go for long walks, exercise profusely, have a long shower (trying to cleanse my esteem along with the rest of me) and then go to bed. Other times I would go straight to bed! The feelings of failure and guilt plagued me. Why was I not able to experience joy in my life?

Trying to manufacture comfort, joy, and peace through our own human standards will always leave us feeling just short of the real thing. It's nice but it's not soul satisfying. The true form of these can only come from God alone.

The fruit of the Spirit is love, joy, peace, patience, kindness, goodness, faithfulness, gentleness and self-control.

Galatians 5:22-23

The fruit of the Spirit is just that, fruit of the Spirit of Jesus Christ that resides in all who call Jesus Christ their Lord. These are creations of God and any reproductions by human standards do not quench the soul like the original! Granted, God bestows these gifts so generously that many people just assume they are built in or achieved by our own efforts, but if you have really tried to create these fruits I know that you will find your efforts frivolous. That is what people find so frustrating about the human nature, we know desperately what we want but we just can't achieve it on our own.

It was a lengthy process, but I had to unlearn the pattern of trying to take comfort in the things I had created as a safe haven, to now 'learn' to take comfort and find my refuge in God. Running to the TV and snack box only seemed easier because I had trained my mind in that way for so long. It had become an addictive habit. The battle was in my mind.

When you are having a 'fat' moment (or a 'stress' moment) what specifically goes through your mind at crisis point?

Now go back and put what should be going through your mind. See if you can use a reference guide to find passages from the Bible to support these thoughts.

Again you must decide who is going to be Lord of your life. The world and what it tells you, your friends, the latest fashion magazine, yourself and all the thoughts that you have or God and his perfect nature?

Verses 3&4: As for the pagan priests who are in the land and the nobles to whom all delight; I said, 'The sorrows of those will increase who run after other gods.' I will not pour out their libations of blood or take up their names on my lips.

When David wrote this psalm, he pointed out that everyone seemed to delight in the pagan priests and the nobles in the land. Granted, I did not live in this period of time but I think I understand why. Things are not so different today. It is much easier and seemingly quicker to follow the latest trends of the day rather than the slower and more thorough route of the Lord. I'm sure in David's day the true priests of God spoke of Godly ideas like peacemaking and humility. These, and other ideas like it, require commitment (a word no generation seems to like) and a passion for God.

When you follow Jesus you will not fit into this world. Jesus said, *'My kingdom is not of this world.'* John 18:36. He explains this further in John 15:18 & 19,

'If the world hates you, keep in mind that it hated me first. If you belonged to the world, it would love you as its own. As it is, you do

not belong to the world, but I have chosen you out of the world.
That is why the world hates you.'

As we are not of this world, we are not to operate in the same way that the world does.

For though we live in the world, we do not wage war as the world does. The weapons we fight with are not the weapons of the world.
2 Corinthians 10:3 & 4

Just because everyone else is doing it and something is the rage of the day does not mean we are to follow in the footsteps of those around us. People may not agree with how you are going about things but just remember you are serving Jesus, not the people around you.

You will always have people trying to give you the 'facts' on how to lose weight, find success and be completely in control of your life. This is subtly concealed in every advertisement, in most educational training and in and throughout our culture. You need to decide right here and right now, are you going to chase after these mirages of success or focus on the one true God who holds the key to your life?

There are so many roads in life that we may choose to follow. When it comes to your life, God wants all or nothing. He leaves the choice up to you but one thing God can not tolerate is sitting on fences.

I know your deeds, that you are neither cold nor hot. I wish you
were either one or the other! So, because you are lukewarm-
neither hot nor cold- I am about to spit you out of my mouth. You
say, 'I am rich; I have acquired wealth and do not need a thing.'
But you do not realize that you are wretched, pitiful, poor and
naked.

If you're anything like me you have run after many different methods and ways to conquer this weight issue. If you had found success you would not be reading this. I can say that when you do it God's way you'll never go back to the place you began. Yes, it is a bit scary knowing that you'll have to stare truth in the face and come to grips with your own human failures. It is a very humbling experience coming to a place where you admit not being in control and that you have many things not very nice about yourself that will have to change, but you will be made new.

Therefore, if anyone is in Christ, he is a new creation, the old is gone, the new has come!

2 Corinthians 5:17

Verses 5&6: Lord, you have assigned me my portion and my cup; you have made my lot secure. The boundary lines have fallen for me in pleasant places; surely I have a delightful inheritance.

Although God has created everything, does God place limits and boundaries on what he has made? Definitely! The Old Testament describes the laws of God's boundaries for humans and in the New Testament Jesus fulfills them, so that in him we find life and everything we need. Because we are created by God we also have boundaries and limits built within us.

There are many physical boundaries designed into our bodies and they include a variety of fun effects, most of which we are not very comfortable talking about. So I will touch upon a few and I think you will get the gist of what I mean. One sign is the color of our urine, when we do not drink enough water it becomes dark yellow and we need to replenish our fluids.

When we eat too much junk food we begin to feel that heavy, sick-like feeling and experience reflux or fluctuation problems. Sometimes if we eat the wrong foods for our body, our skin reacts with everything from rashes to pimples. We can acquire headaches, tummy aches, vomiting and diarrhea if food is not prepared or cooked properly. We may feel faint and shaky if we have not eaten enough or skip a meal. I found that there are many foods that can affect me emotionally and this can be more serious than the physical problems.

There are many different signs and signals built into our bodies. Take the time to get to know your body and its signals and reactions. Experiment with the variety of foods God has created on this earth. We get so stuck into our little realm of eating likes and dislikes that we fail to expand the horizons. You may think you dislike fruits and vegetables when really I would venture to say that you just haven't tried a wide enough variety of ways to eat them.

After eating, take note how you feel. Do you feel energized, comfortable and content? Or do you feel heavy, lethargic and depressed?

The body is designed to let us know we have had enough to eat by our stomachs feeling full. Granted we may have been on so many diets that our stomachs have shrunk and stretched so that we no longer feel the appropriate fullness levels anymore. Ask God to restore the feeling again.

One of the biggest culprits for overriding the physical fullness alert is by eating so fast. I will never forget the illustration God revealed to me on how he feels about this matter.

Imagine on Christmas morning that I handed you a large present wrapped in beautiful, shiny, gold paper with a soft, red, velvet ribbon tied impeccably around the gift. The way that I handed it to you implied that there was something quite valuable inside. The look on my face showed the time and effort I took in choosing the gift for you and the excitement of seeing you blessed by it. Would you immediately rip the paper off in shreds, open the gift and then throw it over your head behind you and shout, 'Next!'?

If we had any appreciation, we would take time to ponder the gift and treasure it. We would think about the person who has given the gift and thank him for taking the time and effort for doing so. Yet look at the way we eat. Here God has designed an amazing array of foods for us and we rarely appreciate it. Do we take time to enjoy our meals, thankful that we even have such beautiful food to enjoy or do we just shovel it in not even bothering to notice what we are eating? Do we eat with a thankful heart, enjoying the taste and smells of our meals?

Why are we always in such a hurry? Where are we going that we have to get there so fast? The most important parts of life involve who you spend it with and taking time to 'smell the roses' along the way. So let's turn off all the distractions around us and learn to appreciate one thing at a time. Let's share some meals with people we love whether it is family or friends and take the time to enjoy the meals we have with them.

'Dear Father
I accept the gift.
I unwrap it, Hold it,
Cling to it, Absorb it.
It becomes part of me.
I become what I was created to be-
Yours' *Sharon Hird*

Look at the many meals that Jesus shared with those around him. Meal times were long and often spent in discussing matters of the heart, sharing and teaching. For those of us who have children, think about what we are teaching them. Do we want them to just shovel down their food or endlessly be eating at fast food outlets? It is because of the hurried way we eat that the full signal often doesn't come until it's too late. As we slow down, our stomachs will have time to actually feel full.

If you look closely in the Old Testament, you will not find a commandment that says, 'You shall eat everything on your plate'. When you feel full, stop eating! I want to break the hold of this old myth right now! The food left over is not going to save a starving nation! Food needs to be sent off a long time before the preparation phase and most starving nations could not stomach the food we eat anyways. After a short time of leaving food on your plate you will start to know how much your body can really handle and you will stop putting so much on your plate. If it really gets under your skin to leave food behind, then freeze it, store it or give it to the dog but stop tormenting yourself over this issue. If other people ignore your pleas to have less food and pile up the food on your plate then it is up to them to deal with the left overs.

There are also biblical limits and boundaries that God has designed for us. Some are spelled out and other lie in between the text. Some people refer to the latter as the 'grey area' of the Bible because these guidelines seem to be non-specific about certain areas of our lives. Take dieting, for example. But the principles that will lead you to success are actually in there. The more we read God's word, the clearer these become.

Pray the Holy Spirit will open your understanding of God's word before you read the Bible and the passages that held no meaning before will suddenly become like beacons of truth and you will start wondering how you ever missed it before. Many times I have read the same chapter, even the same verse of the Bible over and over and gained new understanding and insight each time for various places of my journey in life. Grey areas will begin to diminish the more you read and study God's word. Let's continue on.

Verse 7: I will praise the Lord, who counsels me; even at night my heart instructs me.

The Lord is our personal counsellor who is beside us every hour of every day. You will not be able to find a person in the world who is more dedicated to you and your success than the Lord Jesus Christ.

Although God is with us all the time, it does not mean that we are in the right frame of mind to hear from him. He is able to speak through thunderbolts, I'm sure, but I think he'd rather just have you sit still and listen for awhile.

I love how this talks about God counseling us at night because for most people this is the time we need Him most. I would venture to say that from 4pm on, most people experience the danger zone of dieting. The best laid plans seem to go astray as consuming hunger takes its place. We are tired from the day so it becomes harder to fight off the urges and temptations. It can potentially be the loneliest time of the day even if family surrounds us.

After the sun goes down seems to be the best time to get to heart issues. The still of the night is a soul searching time. Is it any wonder that God would choose to move our hearts at this time. Instead of vegin' out in front of the TV, take some time to get to know your personal counsellor. Read up on his curriculum vitae in his word contained in the Bible. As He instructs you, write it down so you learn it and remember the lessons.

Verse 8: I have set the Lord always before me. Because he is at my right hand, I will not be shaken.

This is the key verse. I have set the Lord always before me. Before who? Me. When? Always. Do you always place God as priority and you next? I remember reading a book called *In His Steps*, by Charles Sheldon, and it tells a fictional story of what would happen

114

if people really did put Jesus first in everything they did. It is a life-changing book. Many times we truly do think we are putting God first when really we are putting our idea of God first. Let me explain through an example from my life.

Many people say grace before eating their meals. Our family started this tradition several years ago to thank God for all of His blessings. We wanted to put God first before our stomachs and learn to be appreciative of all the good things He has done including the meal that lay on the table before us. As time went on, however, I found it was more of a chore than a prayer. It became a bizarre form of penance and I didn't give it much thought. I rushed through it so I could begin eating. God really convicted me about this.

Any time we come before God, we need to understand we are entering a Holy place and are privileged to present our requests before Him. Rushing this time without any thought is offensive to God. If you look at all the examples in the Bible, it is clear that God would rather have pure-hearted devotion than meaningless sacrificial acts. And if like me you worry about the food getting cold then pray at the end of the meal or don't serve up the food until everyone has finished saying grace. It is like every other aspect of our Christian walk; we have to work at making the time for pure-hearted worship and devotion to our Lord.

Do not be anxious about anything, but in everything, by prayer and petition, with thanksgiving, present your requests to God. And the peace of God, which transcends all understanding, will guard your hearts and your minds in Christ Jesus.

Philippians 4:6-7

If you are struggling with food issues, this is a perfect time to ask God to help you overcome. You may want to pray that he show you what to eat or to let you know when you are full. Ask Him to look at your plate and to let you know if He is satisfied with what you have chosen to eat. If you could physically see Jesus sitting next to you would you eat any differently? Well He is next to you so share your thoughts and worries with Him. He will help you overcome all obstacles.

Verses 9 &10: Therefore my heart is glad and my tongue rejoices; my body also will rest secure, because you will not abandon me to the grave, nor will you let your Holy One see decay.

How many diets can you say the same thing about? Have you ever been on a diet where your heart was glad and you were so excited that your tongue literally rejoiced? Well, get ready! You are about to encounter a completely new way of living through the Spirit of God.

Here's a visualization exercise. Picture yourself looking in a full length mirror - naked. As you scan from head to toe I want you to create within you the feeling of satisfaction. Sure there are a few things about you that are different from anyone else but they are part of what makes you so unique. Consent to the fact that you don't look like a super model and become okay with that. Begin to awe over the amazing wonders of the human body. Think of all the things this body has brought you through; from tough times to times of joy. Stand there in your mind until the feeling of happiness appears. This exercise may take some time, so allow for it and don't stop until you get all the way through to happiness.

Don't you know that you yourselves are God's temple and that God's Spirit lives in you? If anyone destroys God's temple, God will destroy him; for God's temple is sacred, and you are that temple.

1 Corinthians 3:16-17

The Bible calls your body a temple of the living God and that we will all give account to how we have handled this temple. How have you handled this temple? Have you looked after it and nurtured it? Have you treated it with the same love and compassion that the priests cared for the temples of the Old Testament? What can you begin to do to look after this temple better?

As you read the Old Testament look at the time and the care the good kings put into restoring the temple of the Lord. 1 & 2 Chronicles detail the temple's care in relation to the heart of the King. For example, read 2 Chronicles 24 and 29. These chapters show a glimpse into the time and effort King Joash and King Hezekiah spent in looking after the temple of God.

Now, I want you to really go to the mirror and say the words of verses 9 & 10 aloud.

'Therefore my heart is glad and my tongue rejoices; my body also will rest secure, because you will not abandon me to the grave, nor will you let your Holy One see decay.'

Say them several times and really let them sink in. Learn what it means to be content in all situations. Be content with the person that you are. It is a choice not a feeling. When the inner man is content the body will eventually align itself accordingly.

Verse 11: You have made known to me the path of life; you will fill me with joy in your presence, with eternal pleasures at your right hand.

God wants to give you more than success in eating. He wants to make known to you the path of life! In him lies the answers and direction that our lives are meant to take. This includes every aspect of our lives.

As a mature Christian you may be wondering why you have not found this contentment in the area of eating and self-image already. Well maybe you've never asked or thought that God was interested in this area of your life. Maybe you have done it your way for so long that there has been no room made available for God to move.

Whatever the reason, our God is the God of new beginnings and fresh starts. Why not resolve to put all of the past (including the bitterness and hurt over past mistakes and failures) behind you and try again, giving complete control to God and consenting to do it His way. 'How?' you say. Read on!

Notes:

Chapter Eight
Listening

Psalm 32 shows a dialogue between a man in need and a loving God. Of all people, David new what it was like to be tempted. He also struggled, ran, tried to hide, feared and even failed many times. Yet David knew where he stood with God. In Psalm 17:8 he says, 'Keep me as the apple of your eye.' David knew that he continually messed up but he also knew how much God loved him.

Take a look at Psalm 139 and you will understand just what I mean. In fact, it is a good idea to read Psalm 139 so you can begin to understand just how much God loves you. He knows everything about you because He created you. There is nothing you can do that will surprise or shock him, believe me, He has seen it all!

I am fearfully and wonderfully made... My frame was not hidden from you when I was made in the secret place... Psalm 139

Yet He still maintains His love for you. He is the God of second chances and new beginnings. He is the God of hope.

Psalm 32 is how to follow the plan given in Psalm 16. In this psalm let's listen to a man who has experienced God and his salvation and the words God has to say in response. Within this psalm lay the keys to success in following the plans of God.

1. Know your goal.

Verses 1&2: Blessed is he whose transgressions are forgiven, whose sins are covered. Blessed is the man whose sin the Lord does not count against him and in whose spirit is no deceit.

Notice the first part of this psalm is not about you doing anything. It is a state of being where God does all of the work. The focus here is on God and what his forgiveness means to us. When God forgives your wrongs it releases you to live, free from the guilt and conviction. This can mean so much to a person who feels she just can never get it right.

The Lord starts off His action plan by giving you the goal first. He does this so you have hope. Without hope there is no reason to begin any journey. There is no time frame to God and He does not have to adhere to a worldly order. He can give you success first. And the outworking of this success will follow in His timing, not ours. If the battle is won in the mind then it has been won altogether.

I do a lot of goal setting. The key to making a goal come to be is to have something to set your focus on. If you can actually visualize yourself as if you have already achieved the goal, you are more likely to attain it. If you see the finish line it gives you hope to get there. The final picture is truly the base to which we hook onto if we are to overcome the doubts and worries within the mind. Here the end result is that we are blessed.

Take a moment to write what it means to be blessed. If you are truly blessed, what does your life look like?

I used to run on the cross country team in college. I have no idea to this day why I chose to enter into such a sport other than it probably helped me to lose weight. As I look back, I just have no idea how I managed to stay on the team for two years! I remember forcing myself to go to training each day and just dreading the first few steps of running. As I ran, I remember having a range of thoughts from, 'I am so sore and this is so hard' to 'I can't wait until I'm finished' and 'where are the toilets?'. But once I finished, I always had a great feeling like I had accomplished something. And if you know anything about me, I had accomplished a great deal.

I think the biggest part of me sticking with it was the great coaching I received. My coaches taught me so much, not only about running races but about running the race of life and persevering with it. The one thing they consistently hounded into my brain was to keep picturing myself crossing the finish line- to imagine it so hard that I could actually feel myself going across it. They always encouraged us to finish what we started. Well, it worked. I always managed to somehow cross the finish line and show up for training everyday for two years. The vision was the only thing that kept me from quitting.

David states the truth of the matter- a man is blessed when he carries no past, no mistakes, no wrongs and no guilt. The only way to accomplish this is through God. We can't erase our past or our memory of it and therefore it is very hard to overcome the guilt and regret that rides along with it. But when we ask Jesus into our lives and ask Him to be our Savior, He stands in front of us, blocking God's view of our sin and failures. God chooses not to see the bad in us because of our love for his son Jesus and His love of his son Jesus.

So if God chooses to forget our past (which, because He is God, He can actually do) then what else matters? Even if we can't forget it, the one to whom it matters most does and therefore guilt should no longer remain an issue. But most of the time guilt does hang around which is why God must go deep to the root of the problem and show us the way out so that we come to an understanding of what he has done and forgive ourselves. God always starts where the problem stems from. He attacks it at the root. There is no point to a surface pruning when it doesn't resolve the deep rooted problem because it will only come to surface again in another season.

I remember a time when I was at the playground and a little girl was falling off the equipment. I lunged to rescue her and after setting her safely on the ground realized that I could not straighten up again. I had pulled my lower back in such a way that it was too painful to even stand up. I thought to myself, 'Oh boy, here we go' thinking of the long journey it was going to take to get me out of this one. As you may have already worked out, this was not the first time that I had pulled something out of place in my body.

Well, I had treatment first and I was able to almost straighten up without pain. A few visits to the chiropractor gave me a bit more movement. After much stretching and walking throughout the following weeks, I thought I was getting close to normal. However, it never seemed to go away completely. One morning I woke up feeling just as sore as I did when I first put it out of place. How aggravating!

I went to an appointment with a sports masseur feeling like I was out of options and had given up hope of ever feeling better again when she did the unexpected. Instead of working on my lower back, she worked on the muscles just below in the gluteus maximus and upper hamstrings. After sending me through the roof a few times working out the knots in those very tight muscles, I got up and walked out of her office feeling completely better.

Why do I share this with you? I am not supporting one method of pain relief over another but I am trying to get the point across that the lower back wasn't actually where the problem stemmed from. When lunging to save the little girl, it was the upper leg and bottom muscles that were strained and pulled from their normal position. This not only fooled me but the many other professionals who were working on me. Once the true source of the problem was resolved, the many other problems surrounding it were also fixed.

Happy are those whose sins are forgiven, whose wrongs are pardoned. Happy is the man whom the Lord does not accuse of doing wrong and who is free from all deceit.
(The Good News Bible)

These verses funnel down to the very key to success with God: the low down, honest, truth with God and with yourself. If you are not operating in the truth and are in denial you will never be able to move from the place you are at. The hardest part about this is that you will not know you are being deceived or are in denial unless the Holy Spirit reveals it to you. None of us want to hear the bad things about ourselves: who we are and how we live. It is very humbling, almost deathly, to face the truth. I say deathly because the old you begins to die as you discover new truths about yourself and move to change accordingly.

2. Operate in the truth.

Verses 3-5: When I kept silent, my bones wasted away through my groaning all day long. For day and night your hand was heavy upon me; my strength was sapped as in the heat of summer. Then I acknowledged my sin to you and did not cover up my iniquity. I said, 'I will confess my transgressions to the Lord'- and you forgave the guilt of my sin.

Notice that confession seems to be a big part of making God's plan work. The confession is really the release of what has to be let go in order to move on. However, the confession in itself is not the difficult part. It is changing the attitude of the heart that moves us to confess that is seemingly impossible. We have a mindset that says, 'Why should I? I don't have to confess' and then the negative thoughts arise about the whole issue of confession.

Again, I return to the classroom for an illustration. When I begin teaching an English lesson to an upper school class I can tell if the lesson will be effective or not merely by looking at the body language and facial expressions of my students. If a young man is sitting with arms crossed, leaning back with a smirk on his face, I know I have my work cut out for me. If I am speaking to a young lady and she rolls her eyes then I know all respect for me and for what I just said has gone out the window.

Probably the biggest thing that I discipline my own children about is their attitude. My little angels can do many things that are wrong or messy but if there is an underlying negative attitude that goes along with it, I get on top of it straight away. Why? Because bad attitude means that they believe they can do things their own way without concern or respect for those placed in authority over them.

I do not want my children to speak back or disrespect authority in the many areas of life including the classroom, their vocation, or even with the law enforcement authorities. If they do there are some very hard consequences including failing a class, losing a job or going to jail. These are just worldly consequences. But when it comes to spiritual matters there is everything at stake. I don't want them to lose a beautiful relationship with our Lord Jesus here on earth or miss out on spending eternity with Him in heaven.

When it comes to bad attitude I speak with a lifetime of experience. Yes, some of it was taught to me but most of it I generated all on my own. It doesn't matter how you acquire a bad attitude, getting rid of it is never easy. It means going back and fixing things you have wrecked and pushing your very highly opinionated opinion out of the way to allow someone else to have the floor for awhile. I have heard God described as a perfect gentleman because He will never push in or come into our lives uninvited. Our attitude is really what determines the invitation for God to speak and move.

3. Get rid of the bad attitude and choose to maintain a good attitude.

Verses 6&7: Therefore let everyone who is godly pray to you while you may be found; surely when the mighty waters rise, they will not reach him. You are my hiding place; you will protect me from trouble and surround me with songs of deliverance. Selah.

The goal may be set firmly in place and the attitude at bay but it all is wasted without the third concept of coming to God. We have ideas of reading God's word, praying to God about these important matters concerning us and taking the time out to listen but none of it will happen unless we make it happen now! I emphasize *now* because this truly is the test of attitude. Coming to God straight away with a determination not to leave until an answer is found shows Him you truly mean what you say. Putting it off until tomorrow already expresses an attitude that it is not your top priority.

If something is important enough, we drop everything to attend to it. If someone close to us falls seriously ill and goes to hospital, we show our concern by leaving the office, canceling appointments, making arrangements for family to be picked up, so that we can go straight to the hospital to support the person we love.

You may be thinking, 'yes, but that is an emergency' and a meeting with God is not? This so clearly shows where you are with God. Do you truly believe in God? Do you just believe that he exists? Even the demons believe that and shudder. See James 2:19. How important to you is a relationship with the living God? Clear your agenda and make some time to work at this relationship. It takes the same amount of effort, or less, to plan a holiday, a day away or even making time to watch you favorite TV show.

4. Do it now!

Once the time has been made then it is time to get serious with God. Praying is the communication line between you and God. Where does one start when communicating with their creator?

Well, certainly we can begin talking to God at any time and in any place. Note that you do not need to pray a set prayer or speak in a Tibetan monk-like voice. Simply chat like you would to a friend or to your father. Sometimes I pull a chair out for both of us and just start talking. Other times I speak to him with the thoughts in my mind or write him a letter in my journal. Talk about anything on your mind. Sometimes we just need to talk things out for our own reasoning and understanding as well. God is always listening so He will hear what's on your mind and in your heart. But don't just end it there with an 'Amen' and hang up!

Like in all good relationships, listening is crucial to getting to know someone. If you were the only one talking you would never really get to know the other person. So often God is actually speaking but we are so infiltrated with worldly matters and the business of the day we forget to actually take the time to listen.

5. Make the time to listen.

I'm sure there are many thoughts flowing through your mind at this point. 'How do I hear God's voice? What does it sound like? What if He doesn't want to speak to me? How can I make Him talk? I am just so little and He is probably too busy running the world to care about my little world!'

The Lord said, 'Go out and stand on the mountain in the presence of the Lord, for the Lord, for the Lord is about to pass by.' Then a great and powerful wind tore the mountains apart and shattered the rocks before the Lord, but the Lord was not in the wind.

After the wind there was an earthquake, but the Lord was not in the earthquake. After the earthquake came a fire, but the Lord was not in the fire. And after the fire came a gentle whisper. When Elijah heard it, he pulled his cloak over his face and went out and stood at the mouth of the cave. Then a voice said to him, 'What are you doing here, Elijah?'

1 Kings 19:11-13

For many years after I first became a Christian I wondered about the many comments other Christians made about hearing from God. They would say, 'God told me this...' or 'God said to me ever so clearly...' It sounded as if God spoke out of a thundercloud to everyone but me. I seemed to get little post-it messages from God through other people or from the Bible. But I never seemed to hear from God directly. The exception being when the minister preached on Sunday, sometimes I felt God took over his mouth to speak directly to me! But I longed to hear directly from God myself. I wanted to have what everyone else seemed to have at the time. Basically, I wanted more.

As the years went by I met many Christians, who like myself, did not hear from God like the other Christians I spoke of. They figured that God doesn't speak to everyone like that and that we should just settle for what we get. So I settled and kept telling myself that was the way it was meant to be.

Then I went on an Easter camp that changed everything. The woman speaking had flown in from the other side of Australia and was absolutely overflowing with the joy of knowing God. She had caught my attention long before any words were even spoken. I'm sure she spoke of other things first but she really hit a nerve when she asked the audience, 'Who here wants to hear from God?'

Well, every hand in the area went up, including mine. She continued by asking everyone to sit silently for one minute and just listen. She even timed the minute on her watch. After the time was up she asked if anyone had heard God speak. Well, people lined up and spoke of the many things God had said in that minute. However, I wasn't in the line. Like usual, I just didn't hear anything from God.

I am so thankful she didn't end there. She had the people return to their seats and the conversations began to settle down. As silence entered the area she continued on: 'Many of you did not hear from God in that minute. I understand because I was like you when this was spoken to me at a conference I attended years ago. I want to share with you my story'. She went on to share how she left the meeting feeling very depressed and upset that she didn't hear from God in that minute, so she decided she was going to sit on the beach (her favorite place to get away from everything) until she did hear from God.

Well, I decided that if she could do it then so could I. After all I had nowhere to go, I was booked into the camp for three days, I just prayed God would speak before it was time to go. So off I went to the beach, as it is my favorite place to go as well. I sat down and said to God, 'Lord, I am not leaving this spot until I hear your voice.' And so I sat.

As I tried to settle my brain, thousands of thoughts flashed through my mind. Everything went through my mind from my past memories to what was happening the week prior to camp and even into where I was going in the future. I kept trying to pull my thoughts back to God but then they would distract me again. Finally, after two and a half hours my thoughts slowed down.

Then I began to notice all of the beautiful scenery around me. Waves were quietly rolling onto the shore. Birds would fly by and dive into the water after their dinner. A few sailboats lingered out at sea. The air was perfect and smelled so fresh. It was not until another hour went by that I realized I was distracted by all of the scenery around me and lost focus from hearing from God. Then my body started to cry out. My bottom was sore from sitting there so long and the breeze was getting a bit cool. My mind turned to thoughts of all the ailments my body has ever been through to just wondering about the body. Another hour went by.

My mind cried out, 'focus!' I was still for a bit and then fantasy came in and I began to imagine life in a different country and what it would be like to live other people's lives. Another hour went by.

'Good grief! Focus!' Suddenly condemning thoughts came in. 'You are a failure at being a Christian; you can't even get quiet to hear God. At this rate you'll die of old age and then you can just ask God face to face when you see him.'

Then the doubts came in, 'Is God really there?', 'Does He care enough to speak to me?', 'Have I done something wrong that God doesn't want to speak to me?' Another hour went by.

Then there was silence. I literally did not know what to think next. I became still.

Be still and know that I am God... Psalm 46:10

Then after six and a half hours God spoke! It was beautiful and I will never forget it. It was not what I expected. It was what I needed. He didn't speak out of a thundercloud, as such, but He spoke in ways that are almost beyond words. I purposefully will not try to explain it because I would rather have people experience it for themselves. It's much better than what I could describe.

Do you want to hear from God? Are you determined to hear from God? I promise you, if you set your mind to not do anything else until you hear from God, you will hear from Him. Before you go let me ask you something, 'Are you really prepared to sit there as long as it takes to hear from Him?' Believe me, I was really questioning at the third hour just how long it could take. What if you had to wait for days? Is it worth it to you? Just how serious are you? God knows your heart better than you, before you set out to hear from Him, I would encourage you to question your heart.

God may not take so long to speak to you or He may take longer. Do not use my example as a guide. You need to travel your own journey here. I simply want to encourage you to take it. Make the time. Book the days in advance like you would a holiday. Arrange it so that you can do it alone. Plan for one day and if He doesn't speak on that day, plan another. Don't give up! Knock on the door until He answers.

Ask and it will be given to you; seek and you will find; knock and the door will be opened to you. For everyone who asks receives; he who seeks finds; and to him who knocks, the door will be opened.

Matthew 7:7

So be earnest, and repent. Here I am! I stand at the door and knock. If anyone hears my voice and opens the door, I will come in and eat with him, and he with me. To him who overcomes, I will give the right to sit with me on my throne, just as I overcame and sat down with my Father on his throne. He who has an ear, let him hear what the Spirit says to the churches.

Revelations 3:19b-22

Why does God seem to take so long to speak? I think the question should be 'Why does it take so long for our minds to get ready to hear him speak?' We have filled our minds with so much junk of this world. A lifetime of thinking patterns takes some time to get aligned to the way God wants to speak to you.

The day after I heard from God I was addicted. I wanted to hear more. So I sat down the next day and you know what? He spoke after just 45 minutes! The next day he spoke after 15 minutes. Then I started hearing Him at various points throughout the day. I had learned to recognize his voice.

The watchman opens the gate for him, and the sheep listen to his voice. He calls his own sheep by name and leads them out. When he has brought out all his own, he goes on ahead of them, and his sheep follow him because they know his voice. But they will never follow a stranger; in fact, they will run away from him because they do not recognize a stranger's voice.

John 10:3-5

We need to continue meeting with the Lord after we hear his voice as the memory of his voice can fade. As the memory of his voice fades it is easy for other voices to drown it out. But the best part about it is that we can renew that voice over and over again simply by spending time waiting. This is what is meant by the phrase, 'waiting upon the Lord'. See Psalm 130:5, Isaiah 30:18 and Psalm 40:1.

As I have continued to wait upon the Lord, He has impressed upon me that the time of waiting is 'Soul rest'. My soul needs rest from this world and as I come to meet with my Savior, I find it. It's as if my spirit has a place to dance again and just be free to enjoy the relationship I have with Jesus. I need it as much as my body needs physical sleep. If I go without it for too long, I become weak, irritated and impatient. I get distracted and off course. With it I find the power to move in the direction God is calling me to live. Mountains are moved and troubles become small as I am empowered to walk on in His Spirit.

Verses 8&9: I will instruct you and teach you in the way you should go; I will counsel you and watch over you. Do not be like the horse or the mule, which have no understanding but must be controlled by bit and bridle or they will not come to you.

As you continually correct your attitude and begin a life of listening for God's promptings, then comes the important act of obedience. This is where the rubber meets the road so to speak. Obedience is critical not only to your success but to your survival.

When it comes to a battle, a wise general in the army would never think of sending an officer into the heat of the battle if he had never even picked up a gun in his life nor ever trained for such an event. When you are on the front line and the battle is intense, it is too late to begin training to fight. In fact, your survival rate is very low indeed. This is why young men and women have to go through basic training and then into specialized training, so they are truly prepared if ever placed in a warfare position.

It is the same in a spiritual battle. The most beneficial training comes from outside of the actual battle, so that you will have the proper skills perfected when the time comes for you to use them.

For example, let's say you are relaxing in front of the television one night. The kids are in bed asleep and your spouse is busy on the computer in the other room. One show starts to flow into another and you find yourself watching a program you have never seen before. It is quite amusing and you find yourself enjoying it. Then a scene comes on that is a bit 'risqué' and it shows something that goes against your godly convictions.

You begin to feel the slightest inkling that if Jesus were sitting with you He would not want you to be watching this. Would you: a) Continue watching the program thinking to yourself, 'it's the way of the world today, it will move to another scene soon'; b) Sit and think to yourself, 'I really shouldn't watch this but I'll read my Bible later and cancel out any memory of it'; or c) Get up and turn off the television?

Let me now put it to you this way, if you cannot be obedient in an area that is not related to the warfare area of dieting how do you expect to have any success in the actual battlefield? God wants you to get up and turn off anything that hinders your walk with Him not for himself but for you! If you can be motivated to get up and turn off the television when it shows something against godly principles, you have a very good chance of being able to resist turning to a box of chocolate when having a bad day. If you develop the skills of living a godly life it will completely prepare you for the time when troubles arise. The problem is that it does take perseverance to do the right thing but the rewards are just so heavenly.

6. Obey.

One of the most effective ways that you can further your training with God is to get grounded in His word. Get involved in Bible studies where you can ask questions and begin to understand the Bible for yourself instead of depending on someone in the church to explain it to you. Read the Bible, listen to an audio version or get creative on the computer with various Christian computer programs and web sites. Visit your local Christian bookstore or get online; you will be amazed at the many ways God's word has been transcribed.

After you begin to understand the Bible, the thing I would most encourage you to do is to begin to memorize scripture verses. This is a fantastic tool because God can then teach you about that scripture in a variety of circumstances. You can't always carry your Bible and when you meditate on one particular bit of scripture God can just expand on it so much more when it is stored in your mind. Later this becomes very effective for fighting spiritual battles.

The Holy Spirit is able to bring to mind scripture when needed but only if there is scripture stored in there to be brought up. Just reading the Bible begins to put the word into your brain but if you have never read the Bible, the Holy Spirit doesn't have anything to work with in emergencies. This is what it means when the Bible is talked about as being food to our souls. Food cannot help your body unless it is put into the system. Once it is in there the body is able to convert it into a fuel source.

Just as a side note, if you have difficulty sleeping or relaxing, meditating on the scripture you are tying to memorize is the perfect cure. It is also perfect in situations where you can't do anything else like in the dentist's chair or in the car during a traffic jam. If you are not very good at memorizing things, there are some excellent music CDs and even kid's CDs that incorporate the scripture verses straight from the Bible, for example, Sons of Korah or Colin Buchan. The one thing I can say about the children's songs is that I have difficulty getting them out of my mind.

Don't worry about it if you can't memorize the chapter and verse that it came from. It is more important that you simply remember the words. The Bible wasn't originally written in chapters and verses anyways. It is helpful in locating the verse in order that you may show someone else or read more about it but it certainly should not stand in the way of you putting God's word into your brain.

When you are in the midst of a terrible day and feeling like a failure because of the way you look, you will not be able to stand strong if you have not adequately prepared for such a moment. So while it may feel like God is ignoring you in this particular area of your life He is most likely focusing on training you in areas where you have already acquired some success, to further equip you and take you to the point where you can eventually go back and fight properly.

This is God. He is so much bigger than what our minds can comprehend which is why He simply wants us to trust Him and follow Him. He does not do it for His ego, He is already God! He does not need us to acquire His position. He does it because He loves you! He actually wants you to have success in every area of your life. You are His child. He created you. Of course, he wants the best for your life but it doesn't mean He will do it according to the way you want it done.

If you never disciplined or taught a child he would most likely end up killing himself. He would touch burning stoves or play on the highway, do anything he wanted if it were left up to him. The wise parent takes the time to teach and discipline a child so he will grow and be a responsible young adult who can face the challenges of life and survive. This seems like a simple concept to grasp but when we enter into the spiritual realm it becomes very hazy and we get so disappointed when God does not act in the specific way we want Him to. We get frustrated with the church and other people who are Christians around us because everything doesn't follow the plan devised in our mind.

Do you know how many times I have seen people leave the church because it is not going the way they want it to? People seem to think the church is there for their amusement. Like a Sunday show or something. And they expect everyone in the church to act and speak as Jesus would.

The church is merely a training ground for the children of God. We are all in training. Not one has achieved perfection. In fact, the only good you see arising out of a Christian's life is the good God has placed there himself. We will not be able to express godly character without persevering through His training.

Church is probably the biggest battlefield in my life, yet it reminds me of a training simulator. The relationships, the battles taking place in the mind and the struggles are all very real but if you stick with it you won't actually die. As in a simulator you may feel very shaken up and all the emotions are running on high but when it's all done and over, you walk out of the doors each time alive but oh so much the wiser! God is training his people so they may survive when they leave the doors of the church; so they can live their week in the world around them prepared with the right skills. This leaves a peace within the heart that only comes when you know what you are doing.

As my husband and I have moved several times we have attended many different churches. Although this example comes from one church, let me assure you that at every church we have attended, we have experienced similar circumstances and trials. When we first started attending this particular church everything started off fantastic!

It was everything we wanted in a church: upbeat music, fantastic preaching and a real mix of age groups. We met many younger couples expanding their families at the same time as us, so we made a lot of friends and had a lot of fun. In all of this I was learning many things but didn't have to actually apply any of the skills I was learning until Lady M ('M' for mystery) came along. We will leave the name out for obvious reasons.

Lady M and I became acquainted through a particular ministry of the church. We seemed to have a lot in common. Before long, it seemed like we had everything in common. We were in nearly every type of group together in the church and out. This was all okay until I began to notice she seemed to be competing with me in each of these groups. It seemed that everything I did she would try and do it better. I thought to myself: 'This is silly. I mean, what is there to gain? There is no prize we are fighting for.'

Nevertheless, it began to unnerve me. Part of me was embarrassed by her behavior and part of me just wanted to win. I am human after all! And I found myself forced into a competition that I did not want to be involved in. The things I had previously confided in her seemed to suddenly be used against me. Granted, this was not a life or death situation but I could not get it out of my mind. I suddenly couldn't stand her anymore. Everything in me wanted to just get away from her. I began to drop out of the groups we were involved in and began to isolate myself from her. I even thought about leaving the church.

Then God began the training simulator exercise. Just for your information God rarely uses the run and hide simulator. It is usually the go-back-and-make-it-work simulator. This is such a painful simulator. The simulator is very realistic, you actually feel like your heart and all the inner organs surrounding it are being ripped out. It takes everything you have to make it through the exercise.

Not only did God want me to continue on in the groups we were in, He wanted me to be nice to her! This particular exercise also required me to pray for Lady M and support her in the ministries she was involved in. He even wanted me to encourage her and mean it! What made this particularly difficult is that she did not reciprocate any encouragement or kindness in any way. As I prayed for blessings in her life, I watched as she received them. She received them abundantly This was so not fair.

This simulator lasted about a year and a half but you know what? I got through it, alive! Not only did we begin to speak again, we actually began to get along quite nicely. For the first time ever we agreed on some things and our relationship improved. Now in this process God did answer my prayers and He changed her quite a bit but I must admit He changed me a lot.

She continued to do things from time to time that irked me but the power behind it somehow got lost along the way and I no longer cared anymore. I could honestly say I would continue to love her in a Godly manner no matter how she acted. Now I am so glad I didn't run away from the problem. By sticking through it I have learned to love those who I thought I could never love. God blessed me for sticking it out through this simulator and as bizarre as this may sound, I would do it all again. If I didn't learn to love someone through our differences in church then I would never be able to apply it to the people I love outside of the church. The more I go through these experiences, the more I grow and mature to be the person God wants me to be (and deep down the person I want to be).

Verses 10&11: Many are the woes of the wicked, but the Lord's unfailing love surrounds the man who trusts in him. Rejoice in the Lord and be glad, you righteous; sing, all you who are upright in heart!

The final step is to simply trust in God and His promises. I love how this is followed by rejoicing and singing. So often we say we are trusting God but we are worrying and fretting so that our faces look like we have just swallowed a lemon. Truly trusting means that all worry is laid aside and joy begins to take its place.

This is the place where God wants us to live continually. Singing and truly rejoicing that no matter what happens, God has got it in the palm of His hand. We become like a child again with worries lifted and responsibility left to a higher authority. We merely have to come when called and obey his voice but there is so much time left for playing, having fun and experiencing life the way it was meant to be experienced. And when we begin to live in such a way, we no longer worry so much about image and it begins a new cycle of events.

7. Trust in God and smile.

When you rest in God and truly give up your worries and your fears, then you are finally operating in faith and God has the freedom to move in and through you.

Notes:

Chapter Nine
Faith

'Have a little faith!' I have heard this said numerous times in a variety of circumstances but I wonder about the meaning behind this phrase. Is it even possible to have a little faith? What is faith? I have heard it expressed to have faith in God, have faith in mankind, have faith in a particular person and sometimes there it is stated just by itself, 'have faith'. It seems more often than not that there is an implied finish to this statement and that is to have faith that whomever is being referred to will do the right thing. To have faith that in the end everything will turn out right and the story will have a happy ending. Right will overcome wrong.

Define 'faith' in your own words.

Faith is

The Bible describes faith as, 'being sure of what we hope for and certain of what we do not see', (Hebrews 11:1)

It follows on in Hebrews 11 giving example after example of faith lived out by the people whose stories are told in the Bible. God's biggest desire is to see his people live by faith. In fact there is no other way to be a Christian. We cannot see Jesus dying upon the cross yet we can be sure that it did happen as recorded. We did not see God creating the human race, yet here we are. We did not see the Lord lay the foundations of the earth yet it continues to defy all the scientists' struggle to offer solutions and answers to its existence.

I cannot see God in a physical way yet I cannot escape him. I cannot explain to my friends how I hear from God in a technical way yet I do everyday. When people try to deny that God does exist, I cannot agree because I converse with him daily. It is like trying to say my father does not exist. Just because he lives in another country than I do and none of my friends and family here have met him does not mean that he does not exist. I know he does because I talk to him on the telephone nearly every week! However, I do recall a time when I did not know that God existed and until I was introduced to him I questioned his existence myself. It wasn't until I took a step into the unknown that God revealed himself to me. And it seems to me that therein lay the key to faith.

In the movie Indiana Jones and the Last Crusade, Indiana has to follow clues to maneuver his way through a trap infested cave to get to the 'Holy Grail'. The last clue tells him to take a step of faith. This so beautifully displays the faith God loves.

Indiana stands on the edge of a cliff looking across to the entrance to the cave which holds the cup he needs to get, but there is a 15 meter wide chasm with a bottomless drop. There is nothing but pure air between where he stands and where he needs to go. Surely he will drop to his death if he steps off the edge of the cliff he is so securely clinging to. With sweat streaming down his face he holds one foot out over the wide expanse and leans forward surely thinking this is the last step he will ever take. As he lunges forward his foot amazingly hits solid rock, an invisible bridge. As he looks down and scatters rocks across the way, what was invisible now lays clearly before him.

I have found every step of my Christian walk to be similar. I don't see. I don't understand. There is no reason to it nor can anyone tell me the solution but when I decide to take a step of faith, God is there every time. And I wonder looking back how I never saw it before. Faith is truly tested by action.

Take some time now to read through James 2:14-26.

What good is it, my brothers, if a man claims to have faith but has no deeds? Can such faith save him? Suppose a brother or sister is without clothes and daily food. If one of you says to him, 'Go I wish you well; keep warm and well fed,' but does nothing about his physical needs, what good is it? In the same way, faith by itself, if it is not accompanied by action, is dead.

James 2: 14-17

You may have heard the saying, 'He talks the talk but doesn't walk the walk'. What you say is really only validated as true by what you do. Saying you'll get around to it is nothing like a die-hard commitment to actually follow through with it. It is the latter that shows someone that you really care.

144

This is true with the Christian walk. You can say you believe in Jesus and even that you are a Christian but unless you are living it out day by day you are only fooling yourself. Being committed to God means committing to every aspect of His being. This involves His word, His church, communication with Him through prayer and practicing everything He teaches in the way you live. If you are not participating in all of these activities the question simply boils down to 'why?'

God is far more interested in your heart than the actual participation in these activities. If you are not reading your Bible, is it because it is illegal to possess one or you find that your version, out of the hundreds that are available, is rather boring? If you are not attending a church, is it because there is no church in the state or country in which you live, maybe you are fellowshipping with other Christians regularly elsewhere or is it because you are harboring a grudge against someone that has hurt or offended you in some way? It is the latter that is offensive to God.

If that person is not a Christian you may be standing in the way of him becoming one and if the person is a Christian you are holding on to bitterness and anger against a child of God. Either way you are in the wrong unless you continue to attempt to love this person and work through it. That means fronting up to church every week and continually praying that God will help you to love this person. If they do not forgive, or hold bitterness and anger towards you, then Jesus will deal with them in His own time and believe me he will, for He is the only one who is in the position to convict a heart and actually change it. Jesus wants first place in your life, a total commitment from you. He loves you and He is totally committed to giving you His best.

We have seen that faith without action is dead but it is also true the other way around. Action without faith is also dead. They are totally reliant on each other. There are so many people that just go through the motions of being a Christian. They go to church and all of the church activities but when the time of testing comes they fall away, full of doubt and embarrassment. They don't make the time to spend developing a relationship with God: talking, listening and just spending time with God. Some might see this as foolishness but if you believe in God there is no other way to get to know Him save developing your relationship with Him. There is no middle ground here as expressed before-God either sees you as hot or cold, for Him or against Him. So going through the motions is really meaningless unless you have committed to developing a relationship with God.

Faith and action working together with God equals the Christian life. It is not enough to just believe in God as James emphasizes in verse 19, 'You believe that there is only one God, Good! Even the demons believe that- and shudder.' Let's put a stop to comments like, 'If God is really God then why doesn't he just take my problems away? He's powerful enough, why doesn't He simply heal me?' Instead of asking God to always prove Himself, let's live like we trust Him. Because although He is powerful enough to do anything, He will not reduce Himself to being our servant performing to our demands.

For God so loved the world that he gave his one and only Son, that whoever believes in him shall not perish but have eternal life.

John 3:16

Many people know and quote this verse regularly as the key to becoming a Christian but the third chapter of John does not end at verse 16.

When you read on to verses 20-21, you find faith and action working together;

'Everyone who does evil hates the light, and will not come into the light for fear that his deeds will be exposed. But whoever lives by the truth comes into the light, so that it may be seen plainly that what he has done has been done through God.'

We can only develop a love for God when we develop a relationship and practice walking in His light. Just believing that God exists is not enough to save us from being a slave to our own sin. It is a relationship with the living Jesus Christ that brings us freedom.

Now let's apply this to the area of your eating and self-image. Which way are you living- with faith, actions or both?

Do you believe that one day you will have a perfect way of eating and living but have never actually started? Or are you forever trying every diet, health concoction and exercise regime that comes your way not taking the time out to understand why you live the way you do?

Have you been going about trying to correct this area of your life without taking the time to ask God what is at the root of your lifestyle?

Do you believe that God can truly heal you of all the pain surrounding this area of your life? Are you willing to work with God through this difficult journey all the way to the finish line? Can you go the distance without giving up on God?

As James points out in verses 18 and 19, there is so much more to God than just believing that He exists. Don't you want more from this life, from yourself and from God? Don't limit God to specific times and places in your life. If you allow Him to be Lord over everything, to literally give up (give it up to God) your whole life to him, He will bless you in ways I could never put into words.

Remember He knows the desires of your heart because He put them there. Just imagine where He can take you, when He takes over the driving. If you are waiting for all of this to make sense to you then you will forever be in the place in which you are at now. Everything starts with little steps of faith that eventually grow into the miracles that come with leaps of faith.

Was not our ancestor Abraham considered righteous for what he did when he offered his son Isaac on the altar? You see that his faith and his actions were working together, and his faith was made complete by what he did. And the scripture was fulfilled that says, 'Abraham believed God, and it was credited to him as righteous,' and he was called God's friend. You see that a person is justified by what he does and not by faith alone.

James 2:21-24

In verses 21 to 24, James gives the example of Abraham being considered righteous for what he did when he offered his son Isaac on the altar. If you have never read this story I would encourage you to do so in Genesis 18:1-15 and Genesis chapters 21 and 22. The heart of this story is that Abraham and Sarah had finally bore a son after years and years of waiting. Now God wanted Abraham to take his one and only son, whom all the promises of God seemingly relied on, to the mountain to sacrifice his life on the altar where the lambs were normally sacrificed. Surely, Abraham was not hearing correctly! Would God really expect him to kill his son?

So many thoughts must have been at war in Abraham's mind. In fact, he left early in the morning so he would not have to explain what he was doing to anyone. But also in his mind was a faith like no other. He knew God gave him this miracle child when everyone else laughed in disbelief around him. He also knew the power of God and that only God could raise a boy from the dead. But was

148

that God's will? As he raises the knife to plunge into his son, God says, 'Wait' and provides him with a lamb from within the nearby bush. The Bible says God credited Abraham as righteous, a friend of God.

Christianity seems to have slipped into some sort of a polite silence.

It saddens me to think that a faith story like this is just lost in our world today. I mean the whole context is lost in our modern day and age that we live in; lawyers and media alike would have a field day with this story!

What we fail to recognize is that Abraham had a relationship with God and heard clearly from God what he was to do. We have lost the art of listening to God. And I don't know about you but I would definitely want to hear accurately from God before I even contemplated an action of such intense faith. And as harsh as this may sound, it seems that Christians just don't have that kind of faith in God today.

I see rare glimpses of powerful faith but Christianity seems to have slipped into some sort of a polite silence. Stories of faith don't seem to be shared or told anymore. People don't want to offend those around them who may not be of the Christian faith yet by being accommodating to everyone, Christians are losing the very thing that makes them so different from everyone else in the world - walking in the obedience and passion of Christ.

When sharing stories of faith with others, there is no code that says other people have to change or even believe them. So what is stopping us from sharing? When I enter the classrooms to teach today, even in Christian schools, the majority of kids have never even heard about the Bible, much less about the stories contained within it. It seems today people want to serve a god that can be contained within the limits they are comfortable with. How can

149

anyone ever grow without change in their lives and challenges to their way of thinking?

Faith is what makes being a Christian so exciting. The answers are not always black and white. I don't always see the path ahead of me nor do I understand why things happen the way they do. But then God steps in and literally blows me away. I can't explain it nor give scientific evidence; all I am able to do is to stand in awe of the workings of an amazing, wonderful God.

Looking back on the story of Abraham we are able to see God working every step of the way. We have the advantage of knowing all along that God will not really take Isaac's life but will provide a lamb instead. We also can see the prophetic vision of Jesus Christ being offered as God's only son for the sacrifice of all our sins being displayed so clearly in this act of Abraham. But I don't think Abraham was granted such clear vision. Regardless of what he knew about God, this truly was an act of great faith on Abraham's part. Only after the lamb was provided was Abraham able to see God at work. Hundreds of years later, Jesus came and fulfilled that prophetic sign and today we are able to understand all that God was displaying in this event.

The point I am emphasizing here is that while God is at work things will not make sense to us. They may become clearer as time moves on and then we have the advantage of looking back. But for some areas of our lives we may never understand why things have or have not happened to us.

We can not expect to understand the ways of God because He is, after all, God. Because of His great mercy and loving kindness, many times God will reveal to us some of the wisdom behind what He is doing but this is truly a gift, not the expected. When you begin to see God at work it becomes an honor just to be a part of what He is doing. To see Him in action truly leaves one in awe of

150

the power and holiness of God. If anyone could explain it he would sit as God's equal.

So if God's ways do not make sense to us, what is it then that leads us to success and 'righteousness'?

Was not our ancestor Abraham considered righteous for what he did when he offered his son Isaac on the altar? You see that his faith and his actions were working together, and his faith was made complete by what he did. And the Scripture was fulfilled that says, 'Abraham believed God, and it was credited to him as righteousness,' and he was called God's friend.

You see that a person is justified by what he does and not by faith alone. In the same way, was not even Rahab the prostitute considered righteous for what she did when she gave lodging to the spies and sent them off in a different direction? As the body without the spirit is dead, so faith without deeds is dead.

James 3: 21-26

Note that next to the example of Abraham's great faith is mentioned Rahab's great faith. (To read the original story, see Joshua 2 and Joshua 6:17, 25.) It does not matter in the eyes of God whether you are the father of a nation or a prostitute! God wants to use anyone who has faith in Him and is willing to be obedient to what He asks.

Faith involves action. It is being obedient to God's revealed will. It does not matter who you are for God to accept and help you. It does not matter what you have done or what sin you are currently living in. We all are sinners and have gone astray from God's will. (See Isaiah 53:6 and Romans 3:22-34) It is the current heart condition that God is interested in. Take a moment to think about the following verses.

The Lord does not look at the things man looks at. Man looks at the outward appearance, but the Lord looks at the heart.

1 Samuel 16:7b

As water reflects a face, so a man's heart reflects the man.

Proverbs 27:19

And you, my son Solomon, acknowledge the God of your father, and serve him with wholehearted devotion and with a willing mind, for the Lord searches every heart and understands every motive behind the thoughts. If you seek him, he will be found by you; but if you forsake him, he will reject you forever.

1 Chronicles 28:9

Blessed are the pure in heart, for they will see God.

Matthew 5:8

So much revolves around the state of our heart. Now take some time to look into your heart. List the reasons why you want to look different than you do now.

Who is wise and understanding among you? Let him show it by his good life, by deeds done in the humility that comes from wisdom. But if you harbor bitter envy and selfish ambition in your hearts, do not boast about it or deny the truth. Such 'wisdom' does not come down from heaven but is earthly, unspiritual, of the devil.

For where you have envy and selfish ambition, there you find disorder and every evil practice. But the wisdom that comes from heaven is first of all pure; then peace-loving, considerate, submissive, full of mercy and good fruit, impartial and sincere. Peacemakers who sow in peace raise a harvest of righteousness.

James 3:13-18

152

Again we return to the heart attitude. What is behind your desire to look different? Are you harboring any envy or selfish- ambition? Do you want to lose weight so you can show others up? Do you want revenge on someone who has made comments to you? Is it to make your husband/mother/boyfriend happy?

As the verse says, 'do not boast about it nor deny the truth'. Take the time to ask God what lies in the depths of your heart. God wants you to move into a freedom so that you are not dependent on what others think or do. This journey is between you and God. Don't seek rewards here on earth.

Be especially careful when you are trying to be good so that you don't make a performance out of it. It might be good theatre, but the God who made you won't be applauding.

Matthew 6:1 (the Message)

I have received earthly rewards and they leave a bitter taste in the mouth. It feels good for a moment but the glory fades very quickly and you are left behind as a 'has been'. I have also received rewards and blessings from God and let me tell you they seem to hit the spot. They leave you feeling good about yourself but not in a conceited kind of way. It's just enough to give you the encouragement you need to keep going. They are like a breath of fresh air. They come so unexpectedly and yet at the perfect time. They bring joy and hope. I can only imagine what the rewards of heaven hold but I do know one thing, I would rather have what the unknown is in heaven than what I already know the world has to offer.

Go through the checklist mentioned in James 3:13-18. Are your motives behind changing your appearance (or the way you want to go about living your life) pure; then peace-loving, considerate, submissive, full of mercy and good fruit, impartial and sincere?

If they're not, you will have a hard time getting God to bless your intentions. I cannot emphasize enough that God does not work according to the system of this world. You really need to take the time to get your head around this. He will ask you to do things that leave your feelings and emotions in an uproar of protest. He will most likely ask you to forgive and be nice to a mother-in-law that has poked fun at your weight for years or to do something completely out of the ordinary in your life.

I will never forget the day He brought me to wear a bikini to an isolated beach despite the fact that a Jersey cow would have looked better in that bikini than me. I think that was one of the greatest achievements in my life and I praise God that no one was there to enjoy the moment with me save my husband and God himself. Prepare yourself, for this is the journey I am talking about. It's adventurous, wild, convicting, provoking and so worth every minute of it!

I don't know about you but I have been a slave to this world and its system for long enough. I'm tired of fighting so hard for joy when my Lord gives it so freely. I like the fact that I can sleep soundly at night and that my future, although unknown, is in good hands. I enjoy the fact that doubts, worries and fears no longer plague me. When I think back on all the diet concoctions I have tried and the horrible tasting things I have shoved down my throat in the name of 'good health' it makes me so glad that I have now tasted freedom.

Are you a slave to something or someone?

Take some time to ponder the following verses.

They promise them freedom, while they themselves are slaves of depravity - for a man is a slave to whatever has mastered him.

2 Peter 2:19

You are all sons of God through faith in Christ Jesus, for all of you who were baptized into Christ have clothed yourselves with Christ. There is neither Jew nor Greek. Slave nor free, male nor female, for you are all one in Christ Jesus. If you belong to Christ, then you are Abraham's seed, and heirs according to the promise.

What I am saying is that as long as the heir is a child, he is no different from a slave, although he owns the whole estate. He is subject to guardians and trustees until the time set by his father.

So also, when we were children, we were in slavery under the basic principles of the world. But when the time had fully come, God sent his Son, born of a woman, born under law, to redeem those under law, that we might receive the full rights of sons.

Because you are sons, God sent the Spirit of his Son into our hearts, the Spirit who calls out, 'Abba, Father.' So you are no longer a slave, but a son; and since you are a son, God has made you also an heir.

Galatians 3:26 - 4:7

It is for freedom that Christ has set us free. Stand firm, then, and do not let yourselves be burdened again by a yoke of slavery.

Galatians 5:1

I encourage you to read through Romans 6.

You do not need to be enslaved to food anymore. God wants to set you free. He holds everything you need. You face a choice to return to the lifestyle you were leading before going in circles or to take a step of faith into a new journey that will grow you, strengthen you and release you to be the person you were designed to be. Jesus is waiting to take His relationship with you further. Let me encourage you to allow Jesus into your heart, not just for a visit, but to reside there in the dwelling of your heart lest you become like the foolish man in Matthew 12:43-45 who left his dwelling unoccupied.

I will share with you with a story I vaguely remember hearing in church when I was young. It is a story based on a true event about a man named 'Blondin' crossing the Niagra Falls chasm. Think about your faith as you read about his.

Blondin, a tight rope walker, set up his rope above the town centre. As he stood on the roof top he announced at the top of his voice what he was about to attempt. He then began questioning the audience below.

'Do you believe I can cross this tight rope with only a pole for balance?'

The people all cheered in agreement.

'Do you believe I can cross this rope unassisted by anything at all?'

The crowd cheered louder, 'Yes, we do!'

'Do you believe I can push a wheelbarrow across this tight rope, unassisted?'

The crowd was wild with excitement, 'YES'

'Finally, do you believe I can push a man in a wheelbarrow across this tight rope unassisted?'

By now the crowd was wildly jumping up and down chanting 'Yes you can. Yes you can!'

'Then if you all truly believe I can do such a feat, who will be the volunteer to climb into the wheelbarrow?' Not a hand was found in the massive crowd below.

Are you ready to be the person who jumps into more than just a wheelbarrow but into the caring hands of a living God?

Notes:

Chapter Ten
Success

By now, you may be thinking to yourself, 'Now what?'

When God revealed this information to me, he made it clear that this information was merely a tool; a shovel to be specific. He gave me the vision of a shovel digging up deep rooted issues, problems and just plain, old junk in people's lives that was interfering with what God wanted to do. As I presented this information to women and men, God would spiritually dig up the things that were hindering His will for their lives.

You may have found that there are issues that God is dealing with that seemingly have no relevance to eating or dieting in anyway. But let me assure you that spiritual seeds can manifest in a variety of ways. For example, in the physical realm we see stress manifest itself in several different ways. Some people experience headaches or stomach aches. Others find they can't sleep at night. Still others go to the refrigerator to begin eating. Well, this is similar to the issues in your spiritual life.

Throughout various times in our lives, issues arise that God wants to focus upon and deal with to mature us and mould us into the people He designed us to be. Some issues are used as tools to grow our character; others need to be removed so they will not hinder our growth in character. When these issues arise, we either deal with them in the manner God has designed or we bury them.

Often we try to run away from our problems, ignoring them or trying to push them aside. But the reality is that problems don't just go away. You may think they have but unless they are dealt with properly, they reside somewhere within as a seed. Spiritual seeds may lie dormant for a while but they are still there. Then they begin growing and inhabiting areas, like weeds to a garden. Many times physical problems arise from issues God wanted to deal with a long time ago. Whether conscious of the problem or not, you simply could not (or would not) deal with the problem at the time and it buried and manifested itself in your life.

A friend of mine, who wrestles with weight and self-esteem issues, came for prayer one day. As we prayed, God revealed to me that there were three areas in her life that needed to be dealt with. Underneath the surface problems that she recognized, lay rejection, fear and shame. As we prayed, God showed me spiritually where these problems seemed to have a hold in her life. Shame seemed to have a collar around her neck. Fear had built a wall around her heart. Rejection had a vice grip around her brain in the form of negative memories from the past. I did not tell her what God had revealed to me.

This is what she spoke out loud. 'I feel like I know that God loves me but it doesn't seem to get past here (pointing to her neck) and into my heart... My neck is so sore and tense all the time... My heart has felt so clamped up, that just last week I saw a doctor because I feared I was in danger of having a heart attack. I just can't stop thinking about the things my family has done to me in the past.'

As a child, she was taunted and made fun of by close family members about the way she looked. No one expects a child to be able to deal with that kind of abusive pressure in any manner, much less a Godly one; however because it was not dealt with it manifested in her life and she found herself struggling with her weight and low self-esteem. Oppressive spiritual problems get a foothold in a person's life because problems have not been brought before God so that He could deal with them properly.

The good news is that you can take these issues before God at anytime. It is never too late. He is the only one who can go back in time, to the root of your problem and deal with it forever. Note that if you are a Christian, you need never fear being possessed by an evil spirit but evil spirits can be oppressive in your life if not dealt with according to the will of God.

Notice that many of my friend's spiritual issues had manifested in a physical way. She was not aware how much of a hold they had on her life. She was a Christian but not experiencing the complete freedom and joy God wanted her to have. Only God could release her from the grip these memories had on her.

The problems she had stemmed from sin somewhere along the line. Some of her own sin may have come into the equation but most likely it was the effects from the sin of those around her, from the abusive behavior she was experiencing and the lack of love and compassion.

You may have heard the saying, 'your sin will always find you out', yes, and so can others. Everyone has sin. You can't escape it or the effects of it.

This righteousness from God comes through faith in Jesus Christ to all who believe. There is no difference, for all have sinned and fall short of the glory of God and are justified freely by his grace through the redemption that came by Christ Jesus.

Romans 3:22-23

'But God demonstrates his own love in this: While we were still sinners, Christ died for us.'

Unless you confess and bring all sin to God and allow Him to wash you clean, your sin will follow you around in the form of guilt, shame or oppression. Any sin kept in dark places will grow poisonous roots into our lives.

Our pastor had a great analogy about sin. He said, 'sin is like a mushroom: if you keep it in the dark and feed it manure, it will grow'. Sin and the problems in our life tend to go hand in hand. You will never effectively deal with the issues and problems in your life if you don't deal with any sin connected to them. Allow God show you how to deal with your sins. Only God can remove the sin in your life and He will only do this if you bring your problems to Him and trust in Him to save you from these sins.

After bringing your problems to Jesus, you then need to wait upon Him and obey. This requires times of stillness and listening and getting deeply rooted in His word. He can show you where the sin of others left off and where you picked up with your own sinful nature. When He convicts you to do something to make matters right again, you need to obedient. This is what it means to walk with Jesus as your Savior. It is a relationship and a journey.

It all lies in the attitude I talked about earlier. If you think you've got it together and there is nothing wrong with you, then you really have no need of a Savior. If you never get past everyone else as the source of your problems then you are placing yourself as the perfect example, instead of Jesus. If you can't see beyond just the problems into where you've contributed to those problems then you've reached the end of the journey and you have nowhere to go. Only God can give us the spiritual vision we need to get past the problems of this world.

God has shown me that people have unknowingly relegated their struggles to being a diet problem. They, at some point, have tried to use food as a tool to cope and it has backfired in a huge way. Satan has caught on and has been using the diet as a distraction so people will not find and deal with the original issues. If they are busy going from one diet to another and feeling helpless and depressed then Satan has won. If you go to speak to others about Jesus, Satan will taunt you with the fact that Jesus hasn't conquered the problems in your own life; so who are you to proclaim anything? If you try to gain more wisdom from God, Satan will put more pressure on you to fulfill all the requirements of your diet, including exercising and counting calories so you will literally have no time left to listen to your maker. You are virtually immobile in the spiritual realm.

Satan has literally controlled most women and many men in the western civilized countries through this means of 'diet'. He has the full support and backing of all the media. Actually, he's done his job so well he can virtually retire because we do such a good job of condemning ourselves and putting the pressure on ourselves to be perfectionists. A diet can get a person so self-absorbed that they fail to think about anyone else, including God. It really is a tool designed to destroy not only you but God's purpose for your life.

A diet and even an eating disorder can seem so harmless and meaningless, but so does all sin. Please note that I am not saying that dieting is a sin because of the broad sense of the word *diet*, but I will say that anything placed before God in priority is a sin. If we could see ahead to the consequences of sin we would never find ourselves in the messes we get into. The very things that seem so innocent and harmless are the very things we need to continually be praying about.

When we can look beyond the diet and start living the life God has planned for us, despite how we look or feel we will begin to conquer what Satan intended to destroy us. If we seek God first, He will guide us in the directions we are to take for eating and living. The key is to seek Him first. As soon as you begin to take matters into your own hands first then you place yourself as Lord and problems begin. This is the pride issue that stops so many from coming to know Jesus as their savior. Can you humbly admit that you can not control this world and when it comes right down to it, that you can not even control yourself without God's help?

During the course of my journey with this program, I have seen women who have had the burden of eating disorders and diets completely lifted off of them. If you experienced a miracle while reading this book, let me encourage you. Do not rest on your laurels and think that's the end of the story. If you do not give the glory to God and change your ways in order to make God first priority in your life then, 'He who gives can also take away.' (See Job 1:21). I have seen both sides of a miracle and let me tell you, those who take God seriously, pushing through the doubts and committing their ways to God, find great satisfaction. Others who use the time to play and don't commit to studying and obeying God's word end up like the man in Matthew 12:43-45.

If you haven't already experienced a low point, you may have one coming up. I am actually telling you this to encourage you. Often in the physical I will feel quite defeated, depressed or at the end of my rope, when in the spiritual God is doing something quite big. It was not until recently that God revealed this to me as we looked back on my historical 'down points' together. Every time I was in one of my low points, it felt like God had left me to just hang tough out there, all on my own. In reality, God was removing something that was standing spiritually in the way of my growth. Even though I have gone through this process probably hundreds of times, I really didn't understand the connection until God revealed it to me.

Why did I not see this before? God showed me that we are living in the natural and so the only things we can relate to these spiritual times are our feelings of isolation, depression, or even being crazy. We don't have enough spiritual knowledge to call it anything else. In the spiritual it is a time of pruning, refining and growing, good things of God. But how do they feel in the natural flesh? Horrible!

Think of how a block of silver must feel going through the refiner's fire before becoming a beautiful cup. Not that a block of silver has feelings but humor me for a minute. If the silver did have feelings, do you think it could understand the artist's plans? 'You're going to do what to me?', it might exclaim. As it is being stretched over the heat of the fire, it would feel isolated ('All the other silver blocks are over there in the corner and I'm the only one going through the fire'). It would feel the pain of the heat and being stretched, it might even be in agony. But when it was all over just think how it would feel being an elegant and beautiful cup. ('Oh, maybe he did know what he was doing all along').

Many women, after the course has ended, will come to me and say, 'I'm at the heaviest weight I've ever been at. When is the weight going to come off?' Some have said I should pre-warn women who are going to take the course that they could possibly see themselves at their heaviest weight. And it is frightening at first. Any first step of faith makes the heart want to leap out of the skin at the terror of endless possibilities. Realize that two things are happening here.

In the physical sense, your body could be in the process of stabilizing itself. If you jump from diet to diet, your body tends to jump up and down in weight. When the body knows that periods of starvation enter into your life, it prepares for them by storing weight in the 'good times'. Your stomach doesn't necessarily know what normal hunger feels like, so don't be surprised that you are eating all the time and that your body is storing on the weight preparing for the next 'starvation'. But persevere! As you continue on, your body will eventually realize that starvation is not going to happen and it will start letting go of that stored up fat. This does take time!

In the spiritual sense, God may need to take you back to where the problem began to show you the correct way of dealing with the problem. You may find, when you think back, that it was at your heaviest weight that you turned away from God's plan and stepped in to take control of your life. Instead of allowing God to begin the process of healing, you put yourself at the throne of your life and did it 'your way'.

Also, please realize that Satan is throwing everything at you to stop you from realizing the truths of God because once you do there 'ain't no going back!' This is the worst that it gets. This is where true warfare begins. Gaining knowledge about defeating the enemy is one thing but putting it into practice is quite another. And it is the latter that wins the battle.

Please remember this is just a matter of time and God is not in a hurry like we tend to be. It can be extremely frustrating in our fast paced world to slow down. But God wants to do the job properly and won't rush it just to please our desires. If we experience success too quickly and the problems have not been dealt with, the same problems may simply shift to other areas of our lives.

For example, a woman who finds success in losing weight but has not dealt with why she struggled with her weight in the first place may have a difficult time with her new success. Suddenly she is lavished with wonderful comments from friends, family and other people around her. She may begin to base her self-worth on these comments. She may find that her problems have shifted to keeping up appearances to maintain her 'new image'. Now members of the opposite sex are starting to show an interest in her that she has never experienced before and other problems may enter in. If she didn't receive love and attention when she was overweight, she may give into pressure to be sexually involved with the men now giving her this new found attention. When the pressure gets to be too much, it is no wonder that she easily slips back into her old eating patterns and lifestyle that she was so disappointed with in the first place.

So what is your game plan? You can't expect to win a battle without one so make one now. Keep in mind the following.

1. You have got to commit to continually let go of the weight thing and trust God.

If you are looking to measure your success by physical merits, I'm afraid you are in for a disappointment. What I am saying to you is that you have already won this battle if you will only believe so. If in the spiritual you are already there it will take time for the physical to catch up.

2. Make time for 'Soul rest'.

The key to your success lies in spending that time waiting upon God to speak to you. If you take the first step God will always meet you. If you have not done the exercise of 'waiting upon the Lord' until he speaks to you, then I encourage you to start here. If you have already done this in the past, I encourage you to do it again. Even if you already know the voice of God, we need to keep returning to this place of waiting upon God for lengthy periods of time. It gives him the chance to speak what is on His mind to you and it keeps His voice from fading away with time.

3. Say 'grace' before each meal, remembering to really pray about the meal and your eating habits in general.

When you pray about the food you eat, God may show you something that seems to be unrelated to food at all. Take the time to pray through this matter, as it may be an underlying cause to the way you eat. Keep your mind open and allow God to show you how the unexpected affects you.

Another matter I will bring up here involves the matter of fasting. This seems to come up in every group I have run. At this point in time, you should not fast. Many people do not understand that fasting from food is like dangling a beer in front of an alcoholic. Until you are completely healed from your eating problem, you should not fast in this way. If you feel serious about praying, God will be happy with you fasting from television or shopping and committing the time to pray and be still before Him.

Does the Lord delight in burnt offerings and sacrifices as much as in obeying the voice of the Lord? To obey is better than sacrifice, and to heed is better than the fat of rams. 1

Samuel 15:22

Therefore, I urge you, brothers, in view of God's mercy, to offer your bodies as living sacrifices, holy and pleasing to God-this is your spiritual act of worship.

Romans 12:1

Remember, God knows your heart and your intentions. If there is an area in your mind that thinks about losing weight, even in the slightest way, you are fasting with a wrong motive. Our first and foremost goal in anything should be on God and His will for our lives, not on any worldly matters.

4. Continue meditating on His word.

Look up the scriptures listed at the back of the book and spend time thinking about them, what they mean and how you can apply them in your life. Memorize as much scripture as you can as it will not only benefit your spiritual growth but keep your mind off temptations to go back to old habits.

5. Make sure you form your very own support team.

Start with someone who is close to you and will journey with you through this time encouraging you. Ask members of your church or Bible study to begin praying with you. This is why God wants us involved in His church so that others will be able to support us and pray for us during the tough times in our lives.

Think about someone who has recently come out of alcoholism. Let's say he has a mandatory work function in a week's time at a local pub. Which would be most beneficial to him; to just go along and hope he is not tempted by the alcohol or to tell some friends what is happening and have them not only praying and encouraging him but actually going alongside with him to the pub?

Likewise, we are not meant to journey through our struggles alone. It is a fact that two or three people are stronger than one; 'a cord of three strands is not easily broken.' Ecclesiastes 4:12. As you begin to share with others about your struggles, you will be encouraged by a second fact: you are not alone. You will be surprised at the amount of people who struggle with issues just like you.

Note that there is a difference between having a support team and an unhealthy dependence on others. You need to meet with God to develop your plan and ask others to encourage you in sticking to that plan; praying for and with you. If you are dependent on others to make that plan succeed, you are in for disappointment. You should only be dependent on God. Likewise God's plans will always involve having unity with other members of His body, other Christians. He will never expect you to journey through life and its struggles alone.

6. If you suffer from an eating disorder, I would also encourage you to seek Christian counsel.

Speak to your minister or another leader of your church to find out exactly who is trained in this area. If you are struggling to find a Christian in the area it is worthwhile to travel to seek this advice. I strongly discourage seeing a non-Christian counselor.

7. Start living your life now!

Stop waiting for the right moment for everything, saying 'one day I'll get around to it.' I would encourage you to do something a bit wild just for today.

As I've stated previously, my very first step to actually living my life was when I went to an isolated beach at the end of summer holidays, so that no one was around. I wore a bikini to the beach for the first time since I was about 10 years old. Even though there was no one else around, for me that was a big step. It was a huge step of freedom and it was just for me and God to share together. It not only boosted my self-confidence but also improved my intimacy with God. Since then I love stepping out and living life as often as possible. It makes life interesting and dare I say, fun.

When God encourages you to do something a little out of the ordinary, He does it for a reason. Doing something out of your comfort zone brings your brain to the right state of mind. It prepares you for times when God may call you to do things that are 'out there' and expects you to obey. Things that come to mind in 'fleeting moments', the ones we seem to shove aside in the busyness of life, are the very things God is probably prompting you to do. This is living life! It is actually meant to be enjoyable!

I hear quite often, 'Am I too old for God to heal me from this?' Never! You are never too old to experience a touch from God. Look at Sarah, who could never have children, trusting God and baring her first child in her nineties! God does not see age so why should you?

8. Go around the problem.

You may experience a physical problem that seemingly is stopping you from experiencing a breakthrough. One woman told me that her bad knee stopped her from walking and that she found it hard to exercise. I asked her if she had thought about swimming instead. Sometimes you need to go around the problem and then you will find that the problem no longer remains a problem in your life. Don't let anything be an excuse to stop you from experiencing success in living life to the full.

9. Begin to expect that your life is going to change.

Expectation in God builds hope and hope does not disappoint us, because God has poured out his love into our hearts by the Holy Spirit, whom he has given us.

Romans 5:5

But those who hope in the Lord will renew their strength. They will soar on wings like eagles; they will run and not grow weary, they will walk and not be faint. *Isaiah 40:31*

God will not allow you to continue in your old habits and patterns of dealing with things. Jesus told this parable,

'No one sews a patch of unshrunk cloth on an old garment, for the patch will pull away from the garment, making the tear worse. Neither do men pour new wine into old wineskins. If they do, the skins will burst, the wine will run out and the wineskins will be ruined. No, they pour new wine into new wineskins, and both are preserved.'   *Matthew 9:16, 17*

When Christ is the head of your life, you just can't live in the same way that you used to. The sooner you get comfortable with Godly change, the quicker God can free you from the bondage of this world. The process goes much quicker when you literally give *up* (to God) and allow God to make the changes necessary in your life to be a new creation in Him.

So from now on we regard no one from a worldly point of view. Though we once regarded Christ in this way, we do so no longer. Therefore, if anyone is in Christ, he is a new creation; the old has gone, the new has come!

                                            2 Corinthians 5:16, 17

10. Encourage others around you who struggle with their weight and self-esteem.

It is only when you reach out to help others in their journey, even though you haven't finished your own; you will find healing for your own life.

Remember this is not the end but rather the beginning of your journey.

And when you do find success and the freedom that goes along with it, continue to be open to God. Always keep every area of your life as an open book before Him. Maintain a willing attitude that always welcomes what Jesus has to say to you and be quick to obey his instruction. If you do you will receive freedom and blessings in every area of your life.

From this point, it is your turn. I have told you all God has commanded me to tell. From here, He wants to take you on the journey He designed for your life. Only He can fill what gaps have been left open by this program. But this is a journey that you have to walk with God on your own. Take the time needed to get to know God. Persevere. Don't give up. Keep asking, persisting, reading, studying, and praying, until you find what you seek. God is faithful to His promises. And He promises if you seek Him, you will find Him. I speak as one who knows. There is nothing better than the freedom that comes from a relationship with Jesus Christ.

Notes:

174

Chapter Eleven
Partner Support
By Marla & Mark Jones

'My dove in the clefts of the rock, in the hiding places on the mountainside, show me your face, let me hear your voice; for your voice is sweet and your face is lovely. Catch for us the foxes, the little foxes that ruin the vineyards, our vineyards that are in bloom,' Song of Solomon 2:14-15

Beauty is more than skin deep. As Solomon portrays in his verse above, there is something comforting in hearing his wife's voice and seeing her face that makes him feel at home. She is his treasure in amongst the rocks of life. Yet he warns there are little foxes that have to be addressed or they could potentially ruin the vineyard of marriage that the bride and groom are working so hard to maintain.

'Husbands, love your wives, just as Christ loved the church and gave himself up for her'

Mark and I felt that it was necessary to write this chapter to give husbands a better understanding on the importance of supporting your wife generally but especially during this journey of healing. If your wife has asked you to read this chapter, please give it go. It means that she loves you and needs your help to conquer issues of weight, image or a lack of self-confidence.

Being a Christian man is a high calling. It means that you take your responsibility as head of the home very seriously. So seriously, that like Christ, you would lay down your life in order that your wife can flourish. (See Ephesians 5:25) The following tips are based on

175

precepts laid down by God, but even if you're not a Christian, we hope you will find the following helpful and practical.

1. Look outside of yourself and make a gesture of support.

The biggest way you can help is to want to help. If you don't know how to help ask God to give you some ideas. Ask your wife how you can help her and really try to listen and implement what she says.

This journey is not going to happen overnight but without your help it may not happen at all. Whatever stage of life you are at it should be never too late to change. Remember that your wife is trying to do exactly that and needs your support.

2. Watch your Words

Hurtful words tear down self-confidence. The lower the self-confidence the more difficult it is to overcome issues that deal with weight. Rude comments are cruel and couldn't possibly help the situation. Even attempted humor or wise cracks often produce the opposite effect.

It is well known that if you continue to tell a child he is stupid, he will think he is stupid. Likewise, if you (or others) continue to tell your wife she is fat, ugly, worthless, etc. she will think she is those things. If you want a beautiful, loving wife, tell her that she is exactly that! You are not lying as she is already beautiful within. Comment on her character as that is far more valuable and lasting than physical appearance. Sometimes we simply have to tell the truth in advance and wait for her to catch up.

When husbands make harsh comments on eating habits their words are suffocating and abusive. It will produce negative effects in
176

women. Some will rebel with secret food supplies. These secret supplies are often worse, as the whole pack of biscuits must be eaten in one sitting so as to hide all the evidence! This downward cycle just makes everything worse and causes women to withdraw inward destroying relationship.

Your words say tenfold about who you are as a person. The people around you that hear your critical words about her weight being said in the public arena are not cringing at her; they are cringing at you and your rude behavior.

If a woman is continually abused verbally by your put downs, please know that she will most likely be encouraged to leave the relationship by local government, community and church support groups until the abuse stops. Verbal abuse is just as serious as physical abuse. If you feel out of control, please seek counseling from one of the many support groups in your local community.

So not only watch your words, stop the hurtful words of others. If you see family members saying things about your wife, ask them to stop. If they continue, get her out of there! Discuss any issues in the privacy of your own home. When you are in public places, you are her rock and you need to solidly support her.

3. Focus on relationship

You may have heard that not many people on their death bed say, "I regret I didn't work more" or "I wish I would have bought more stuff." Life is about relationship and what better investment than to spend time encouraging your best friend, your wife.

Recreation time is needed to refresh and restore our mind, spirit and body. Life is meant to be fun. Busy wives need to be reminded of this often!

It's important to have time set aside each week for time together as a couple, like a "date". This time can be dinner or a coffee, but it could also be a walk, a game of tennis or other fun activities together where you can talk together as you go along. Most women need to feel emotionally close before they feel the physical attraction desired by their husbands.

When you are with your wife, especially on a date, be with your wife. Don't keep checking the football scores or your Facebook account. This demonstrates that the phone or television is more important than your wife and even though you spent time together you weren't really there.

I found it so important to offer my wife time for herself. Many times, I have to literally make her stop and spend some some time having fun. This refreshes her and in turn, refreshes our relationship. If I take the focus off of what I want and put that into building her up, I find I end up with much more time with my wife anyways. And she's happy!

4. Help her live a balanced life.

Men, need to support their partner in all areas of their life including spiritual, emotional and physical needs. How is this done? Well there is no set formula and it's not the same every day. Just when you think you have got it right you will need to change and approach things differently. Never rest on what you have done. You can't coast or cruise along because you will in fact become stagnant and start to slide down the mountain and go backwards.

Our wives are under a lot of pressure with expectations from work, society, friends and Facebook to do it all and to do it well.

Physical exercise is no doubt important. But maybe we need to relook at our exercise. Is it fun? Is it achievable? You don't need to

178

pay hundreds of dollars join a gym. Simple things like taking walks together and planning a bike ride not only get our bodies moving but allow time for relationship building.

Physical needs involve more than just exercise. Help with the grocery shopping. Buy healthy fruit and vegetables instead of junk food. Maybe you could support your wife by learning to cook a few healthy meals to give her a break from always having to be around food. Simply cleaning, chopping and preparing fruit and vegetables or healthy snacks can help ease the temptation to turn to junk food when you are hungry.

Emotional needs can also include mental and social needs and it will be necessary for your wife to have a close female friend to talk to and work through issues. It is well known that most women have a quota of words they must say each day. If your wife has had a bad day and has not talked to one of her friends about it, be prepared to listen for a long time. You don't need to solve the problem or understand exactly what she going through. Just acknowledge that you hear what she is saying and assure her you are there for her. God created men and women differently and as men we are often oblivious to the emotional rollercoaster and issues women are challenged with daily.

Men, we have been called to be the spiritual leader of our family. Pray daily with and for your wife and children and get into the service or ministry of your local Church that God has called you to and use the gifts he has given you. If you are not spiritual, don't deny your wife and children that amazing experience.

Have nothing to do with godless myths and old wives' tales; rather train yourself to be godly. For physical training is of some value, but godliness have value for all things, holding promise for both the present life and the life to come.

1 Timothy 4:7-8

5. Don't Judge Others

It's ok to be concerned about someone's eating habits if you truly are concerned. But watch out for judgmental attitudes that can so easily slip in behind our concern. Who are we to judge?

This is one matter that God speaks about very clearly in the Bible.

Do not judge, and you will not be judged. Do not condemn, and you will not be condemned. Forgive, and you will be forgiven. Give, and it will be given unto you.

Luke 6:37-38

Let anyone of you who is without sin be the first to throw a stone ...
John 8:7

There is only one Lawgiver and Judge, the one who is able to save and destroy. But you- who are you to judge your neighbor?
James 4:12

You, therefore, have no excuse, you who pass judgment on someone else, for at whatever point you judge another, you are condemning yourself, because you who pass judgment do the same things. So when you, a mere human being, pass judgment on them and yet do the same things, do you think you will escape God's judgment?

Romans 2:1&3

One person's faith allows them to eat anything but another, whose faith is weak, eats only vegetables. the one who eats everything must not treat with contempt the one who does not, and the one who does not eat everything must not judge the one who does, for God has accepted them.

Romans 14:2-3

180

Take a good look in the mirror at yourself, I doubt you'll see perfection. But even if you do, realize, it's only a matter of time. As you age, your body will change too, and the compassion you show now to your wife will be most likely the compassion measured out to you.

Finally

Being married and having a family doesn't mean that we have to give up everything, but it would be naive to think that a relationship is one sided and selfish without sacrifices. To me, marriage is the union of two people that complement each other and bring the best out in each other. I still enjoy watching a football game or getting on my computer but it is now in moderation. Now God comes first, then my wife and kids and the rest is a priority down the list. Remember to give glory to God in everything you do, including loving your wife and providing the positive support that she needs.

Try and provide freedom for you wife and not negatively comment or judge her on her physical appearance. This not only includes what she is wearing and how she looks, but also what and when she may be eating. Allow God to move and convict. Do not judge. The physical change in relation to improving self esteem or becoming free from the bondage of food and weight loss or gain will usually not happen overnight. But it can happen with love and support from you.

It has been amazing to see God release my wife from the worldly pressures of weight loss, being obsessed about what she ate and worrying about her physical appearance. Now she doesn't have to hide or worry about want she eats and, in doing so, she has lost weight, feels great and looks fantastic. I'm so glad that I was a part of the healing process in her journey.

Pocket Checklist for Men:

Have I:

*spoke encouraging words to my wife today?
*made one comment today on the beauty of my wife's character?
*been a rock for my wife in stressful situations, standing up for her?
*asked God how to help my wife today?
*asked my wife how I can help her today?
*planned our date night this week?
*given her some time to herself?

Notes:

Chapter Twelve
Church Support

So I am proposing a radical idea. Let's change things up and be different than the world around us as a church. I would like people to be able to come into the church for help with eating related issues rather than having to pay to go to some diet centre. Our God holds answers for these people. Imagine, if everyone who had an issue with dieting, self-image or weight related issues came into the church. We would have to build colosseums just to hold everyone.

So as part of the church, how can we help?

Well the first way is to understand the way God looks at dieters, food addicts and overweight people. Hopefully you would have read this book and have a new insight into these matters. If not, I would encourage you to go back and read this book. If you don't have food related issues in your life, that's okay. The principles taught in this book are helpful in overcoming just about anything.

It is a well known fact that if you attend church or church-related events, you will encounter a lot of gatherings around food. This is meant to be fun. So I would encourage you that when you attend these events, be a part of making it fun for people.

Get the focus off of food and onto relationship with each other. Find out about the people around you and get to know them. Don't always go to the same circle of friends. Branch out and make a commitment to meet one new person at each event and really try to get to know them. If someone looks out of place, make it your job to get them in place. Relationship breaks down many walls and begins healing in people. Taking time out to get to know people and to encourage people is what Christianity is all about. Look at Jesus, what else did he spend time doing? It was all about people, teaching people, loving people and healing people.

When you are at food related events please watch what you say about food. Please be aware that other people around you are listening to your words. What impact are you having on the younger generation of girls? What are you teaching them with your words? Are you grateful for the food that has been served; showing appreciation for the time and effort that has gone into its preparation.

When you say things like, "Oh, that is just wicked!" or "We really shouldn't be eating this," you are degrading what has been placed before. Next time words like that come out of your mouth, have a look at the chef or the caterer's face. I believe it will reinforce what I am saying here.

What other area of life do we announce that we are about to rebel against something openly in front of everyone? "I shouldn't eat this" but then you do. It's like announcing "I shouldn't steal" but then doing it. Or announcing, "I shouldn't gossip but" and then proceeding to do just that.

If you feel convicted by God that you shouldn't eat something then don't openly announce it and then make matters worse by actually doing what you just said you shouldn't do. Simply don't eat it and keep your mouth shut. Your words are killing the self-image of our next generation. When we go to a church gathering where there is food, let's appreciate it. Let's endeavor not to say one negative thing about it all night.

If you have negative thoughts, please keep them to yourself. I also want to challenge you that if you are on a diet, then keep your views to yourself. What works for you does not necessarily work for others yet often I hear women preaching it with more compassion than the word of God. I don't think I can stress this enough, please do not tell others about the various diets you have tried or the current one you may be on. I know this seems harmless but let me assure you that it is subtly undermining God's word and reaffirming what the world system is teaching.

I have always been of the firm belief that you really shouldn't give your opinion about much in the ways of weight, parenting, single status, people's death, etc. unless you're asked and even then, pray first and choose your words wisely. Do not give cliched responses when you don't know what to say. It just grates on people's emotions and drives people away from the church.

If someone one is bigger than you and comes to visit the church you don't need to announce their size to others. Most people can see for themselves. Trust me if a person is overweight, they know it.

When someone comes into the church with weight issues (or for that matter any issues), instead of forming a judgmental opinion, let's commit to praying for them. This is something that you can quietly commit to without telling anyone and you will be rewarded greatly by God.

Be careful about praying in groups, nothing is more disheartening to God than the gossip prayer circle. This is where a group of women get together to "pray" about "Judith's weight issues".

It goes something like this, "Lord, please help Judith not be so offended when I offer advice to her about losing weight. I pray she leaves some cake behind for other people after Bible study today.

Please help her husband and kids not to be embarrassed by her weight when they are in public." If you think that it is important to judge them, then you better be prepared to have all of your flaws judged.

Instead let's pray for Judith in a way that is pleasing to God. It may go along the lines of, "Lord, I pray for Judith. I pray that she will grow in her faith and grow in her journey with you. Please work in her life, bringing healing and use her experience to help others. Protect her from the attacks of the enemy. Help me to love her and speak words that will help encourage her. Bless her abundantly." Use the scripture at the end of this book as a guide to help you pray for the people struggling around you.

No matter if a person has different skin color, a disability, a weight issue, or anything that is different than what we are used to, we need to look beyond the outward appearance and get to know the person. Anything else is contrary to what Jesus taught and lived.

Do you not know that you body is a temple of the Holy Spirit, who is in you, whom you have received from God? You are not your own; you were brought at a price. Therefore honor God with your body. (this includes your mouth)   *1 Corinthians 6:19*

Notes:

Hungry for Life
Scripture Verses

Genesis
2:15-17 free to eat from any tree
3:1-8   Eve and the serpent
Psalms
Chapter 16 The Plan
Chapter 32 How to follow the plan
63:1 You, God, are my God
139:16 Your eyes saw my unformed body
Proverbs
3:8 This will bring health
4:22 They are life & health
5:11 (The body is temporary)
14:30 A heart at peace gives life
Ecclesiastes
11:10 Banish anxiety
Matthew
6:22-23 eye the lamp of the body
6:24-34 do not worry about your life
10:28 do not be afraid
13:7 seed fell among thorns
13:24-30,37-43 (story of the farmer)
26:26 Jesus took bread

26:41 Watch and pray
Mark
5:29 she was freed from suffering
7:19 Jesus declares all food clean
Luke
8:5-8,11-15 Parable of the Seeds
John
10:7-18 The thief and the shepherd
Acts
2:26 Therefore my heart is glad
Romans
6:6-23 for our old self was crucified
7:4 you belong to another
7:14-25 I do what I do not want to do
8:10-13 the spirit gives life
8:38-39 nothing can separate us from God's love
12:4-6 we are members of one body
12:17 do not repay evil for evil
Chapter 14 Do not judge

I Corinthians
5:6-8 get rid of the old so you may be new
6:12 not everything is beneficial
6:19-20 your body is a temple
7:4 yield to each other in marriage
8:8 food does not bring us near to God
9:27 make my body my slave
10:16 the cup and the bread
10:24 no one should seek their own good
10:33 I am not seeking my own good

Galatians
3:26- 4:7 you are all one; you are God's child
5:1 Christ has set us free

Ephesians
4:27 do not give the devil a foothold

James
2:14-26 faith vs. deeds
3:13-18 two kinds of wisdom
4:7-10 submit to God, resist the devil

1 Peter
5:7-8 be alert and of sober mind

2 Peter
2:19 people are slaves to whatever has mastered them

Hungry for Life
Study Questions

The Journey

Read Genesis 2:15-17

'You are free to eat from any tree in the garden';
What do you think it would be like to live in the 'Garden of Eden'?

_____

_____

_____

_____

Continue reading Genesis 3:1-8

What is temptation?

_____

_____

_____

_____

What do you think Eve was feeling/thinking to give into temptation in verse 6?

_____

_____

_____

_____

_____

Why do we want what we do not have?

_____

_____

_____

_____

List the things that tempt you.

_____

_____

_____

_____

If you gave into temptation continually, what would happen?

_____

_____

_____

_____

Describe how you think Eve visualized the fruit of this tree in Gen. 2:17 and compare this to how you think she visualized the same fruit in Gen. 3:4-6.

_____

_____

_____

_____

_____

What happened immediately after Adam and Eve ate the fruit?

_____

_____

_____

_____

What kind of wisdom did they acquire?

_____

_____

_____

_____

Gen.2:17 and 3:3- God stated 'For when you eat of it, you will surely die.'
Did Adam and Eve die when they ate of the tree?

_____

_____

_____

_____

Outline all of the consequences of their decision to eat of the fruit.

_____

_____

_____

_____

_____

Outline all of the consequences you would face if you gave into the temptations you've listed above

_____

_____

_____

_____

Is dieting a spiritual issue?

_____

_____

_____

_____

List the issues.

_____

_____

_____

_____

_____

_____

The Core

If you had to sum up the purpose of your life in a sentence, what would it be?

_____

_____

_____

_____

Are you totally committed to anything or anyone? Explain

_____

_____

_____

_____

Read Matthew 6:24- 34

v.24 What do you think Jesus means when he talks about 'serving a master'?

_____

_____

_____

_____

v.24 What things pull at your servant hood to God? (Or stops you from serving God all together?)

_____

_____

_____

_____

v.25 What does it mean to worry?

_____

_____

_____

_____

In relation to food and drinking, what specifically do you worry about?

_____

_____

_____

_____

v.25   Which is more important to you- life or food? _____

Don't worry about things- food, drink and clothes. For you already have life and a body and they are far more important than what to eat and wear.' (Living Bible Trans.)

197

What is the purpose of food?

_____

_____

_____

_____

Are you preoccupied with food? Where is it in the priorities of your life?

List your priorities 1 to 10 in life. (You may need 2 lists, one in principle and one in practical.) In making this list, it might be worth thinking about what you spend most of your time on, as we tend to spend time on things or people we value.

_____	_____
_____	_____
_____	_____
_____	_____
_____	_____
_____	_____
_____	_____
_____	_____
_____	_____

v.30 Why is this a faith issue to God?

_____

_____

_____

_____

v.32 Does God know what you need in order for you to be happy with your life?

_____

v.33 Write this verse out.

_____

_____

_____

_____

Are you continually taking over th s 'section' of your life, trying to control this in your own way, by your own means?

_____

_____

Do you trust God enough to hand over the whole area of dieting to him?

_____

_____

_____

Heartbreakers

Consider Romans 7:14- 25

Can you relate? Explain.

_____

_____

_____

_____

As we consider the following passages and learn more of God's ways, note at least one way the devil is working in opposition.

Read Matthew 13:24- 30 & 13:37- 43 The Parable of the Weeds

Put yourself in the shoes of the farmer: You've worked hard sowing expensive seed and you are expecting a harvest of good wheat. How do you feel when you see that at harvest time next to every good sprout there is a weed growing, purposefully placed there by someone who does not like you. Describe your feelings.

_____

_____

_____

_____

_____

_____

Now relate those feelings to your life. You have tried so hard and worked like mad to do the right things- what weeds have popped up in your life? How do you feel about this?

_____

_____

_____

_____

Is it just an accident that weeds are in your life? _____

v. 29 Why doesn't God answer a prayer of 'Please God, just take

___(the problem)___ away'?

_____

_____

_____

_____

What 'good wheat' could God be trying to sow in your life through your weeds?

_____

_____

_____

_____

_____

v. 41 Will there be a time when God does take away the problem?

_____

Read Luke 8:5- 8,11- 15 The parable of the sower

Relate this parable to what God may be saying to you in your times of trouble.

_____

_____

_____

_____

What are the things that come and take His word away directly?

_____

_____

_____

_____

List the ways you make God's word take 'root', so that you may flourish and grow in His freedom.

_____

_____

_____

_____

Read 1 Peter 5:8

How does the lion roar in your life?

_____

_____

_____

_____

How do you resist the roaring lion?

_____

_____

_____

_____

Read John 10: 7- 18

Compare the qualities of the Good Shepherd with the characteristics of the others mentioned in this passage.

_____

_____

_____

_____

Read Revelation 12 and from the passages above, summarize the ambition of the devil. Don't forget the ways to overcome! James 4:7- 10, Eph. 4:27, Rom. 8:38

_____

_____

_____

_____

_____

_____

Accountability

Do you view others according to weight issues? _____

What criteria do you place on yourself to be what is in your mind 'acceptable'?

_____

_____

_____

_____

_____

What things arouse anger or envy about the way others are eating around you? Confess this to the Lord.

_____

_____

_____

_____

Read Romans 14

v.4 Have others looked at you in judgmental attitudes about your weight? Having read this passage how should you respond to this?

_____

_____

_____

_____

v.6 No matter what you eat, how should you eat it?

_____

_____

_____

_____

v.7 Are you trying to resolve this issue alone?

_____

_____

v.12 We know that the body is a temple of the Lord. (1 Cor. 6:19) If you were taken today and had to give an 'account' of how you handled this temple, what would you say?

_____

_____

_____

_____

v.13-15 How can we help each other?

_____

_____

_____

_____

_____

v.16&22 Do you find yourself saying things to others like, 'You'll pay for that tomorrow', 'a moment on the lips' or ' you are what you eat' etc.?

_____

v.14 (Mk 7:19) Is there any food that is 'off- limits' by God's standard?

_____

_____

v.23 So if food is not sinful, what is?

_____

_____

_____

_____

v.20 How could you destroy the work of God for the sake of food, in others and in yourself?

_____

_____

_____

_____

_____

Listening

When things just get to be 'too much' and you're not having a very good day, what do you do to comfort yourself?

_____

_____

_____

_____

When you're having a 'fat' moment what specifically goes through your mind?

_____

_____

_____

_____

Do you enjoy dieting? Why or why not? (Specifics please!)

_____

_____

_____

_____

Read Psalm 16

Although God created everything, does God set limits? (1 Cor.6:12)

_____

_____

What are some ways to know God's limits for you with food?

_____

_____

_____

_____

Reading v. 5 -11 as 'God's diet', what are some differences between this diet plan and other diets you have tried?

_____

_____

_____

_____

v. 9 -10 Does God want you to be happy with your body? _____

Visualize yourself saying these words found in verses 9- 10 - How do you look?

_____

_____

_____

_____

Could you speak these words now and trust God to fulfill his promise?

_____

v.7 How can you know the Lord's instructions?

_____

_____

_____

_____

Read Psalm 32

What are the keys to hearing the Lord in this psalm?

1.

2.

3.

4.

5.

Apply these keys to dieting and be specific to where you are right now.

_____

_____

_____

_____

v.6 How do you pray?

_____

_____

_____

_____

v.10 Do you trust the Lord? Can you comprehend the Lord's 'unfailing love'?

Read Psalm 139

209

Success

Read James 2: 14 – 26

What is faith?

_____

_____

_____

_____

v. 17 Why is faith without action considered 'dead'?

_____

_____

_____

_____

Is it also true that action without faith is 'dead'? Explain.

_____

_____

_____

_____

Which way are you 'dieting' – with faith, actions, or both?

_____

_____

_____

_____

v. 18- 19 Is believing that God exists enough to save you from being a slave to your sin?

_____

_____

v. 21- 24 The ways of God don't always make sense to us. When faith and actions work together faith is made complete and you will be credited with righteousness. You will call God 'friend'.

What is it then that will lead us to <u>success</u> and 'righteousness'?

_____

_____

_____

_____

v. 23 Does it matter who you are, for God to accept and help you? (See also 1 Sam. 16:7, Prov. 27:19, 1 Chron. 28:9, Matt. 5:8)

_____

_____

List the reasons why you want to look different than you do now.

_____

_____

_____

_____

Read James 3:13- 18

Is there any envy and self- ambition in the way you 'diet'?

_____

_____

_____

_____

What do you need to change in order to go about God's way of living free from diets?

_____

_____

_____

_____

Have a look at this issue of 'slavery' vs. freedom at home and meditate what God has to say to you. Read 2 Peter 2:19, Galatians 3:26- 4:7, 5:1, Romans 6:6- 23.

Are you living in slavery to this world or are you living in the freedom that God has to offer?

_____

_____

_____

_____

212

Bite of Life
Top 10 Mistakes of Dieters

1. Thinking that a diet is only for a certain time (ex. until weight is lost)
2. Thinking a different diet will do the trick
3. Not being realistic about weight, height, age, post-children, lifestyle, etc.
4. Thinking a 'diet' has nothing to do with God or the Bible
5. Thinking that I can control this on my own.
6. Simply making incorrect choices
7. Misunderstanding the body's design and the way it functions.
8. Resolving problems and issues with food and looking for happiness and comfort in food
9. Forgetting to be joyful and thankful for the blessings in life
10. Depending on a scale or other people's opinions to determine self-worth.

100+ other things to do besides eating

(with room to add more!)

Dance
Have a twenty minute nap
Take a long bubble bath, with a good book and a
    candle
Walk the dog or volunteer to walk a friend's dog
Play with a pet
Watch a goldfish or aquarium full of fish
Light a candle and listen to music
Walk in a local park
Go to a museum or the zoo
Go see a movie
Spend time listening to God
Memorise a Bible verse
Play a board game with someone
Check out the local volunteer centre
Volunteer to help someone in your own way
Pray for someone and then write them a letter of
    encouragement
Talk to a friend on the phone
Pamper yourself- paint your nails, buy a face mask or a
    hair color
Go to the hairdresser
Clean one room of your house
Clean the pantry
Call your mother (or another family member)
Have a cup of tea and relax or a cuppa and a chat
Get a fake tan
 Sit in a solarium, spa bath or sauna
 Go bird watching

Learn something new
Paint your toenails different colors
Cook a meal for a friend (if you're strong enough to
   resist taste testing)
Read a novel
Memorise a poem
Watch a DVD or go to a movie theater
Keep a journal
Read a child a story
Meet a new friend
Go bowling
Challenge someone to a game of tennis or table
   tennis
Go for a swim at the pool or beach
Try an exercise class at a local gym or off of a video
Have a massage
Cross stitch, knit or sew
Paint a room
Rearrange the furniture
Go shopping
Plant a herb garden
Pot a plant
Visit a travel agency and dream a little
Sign up for a local tour
Do a historical walk of your city or a city close by
Try new walk paths around your city or suburb
Walk along the beach
Build a sand castle
Go kayaking
Go snorkeling and swim with the dolphins or fish nearby
Go for a bike ride
Visit someone in a hospital or nursing home
Adopt a grandparent
Surf the net (if you don't have a computer try the local
   library or an Internet cafe)

Go horseback riding

Plan a date with your spouse or a friend

Plan a party

Write a list of goals and steps to achieve them – Then start!

Write an e-mail or create a web site

Go on a Christian chat line or join one of the several outreach programs on the net that train you how to reach out to others and share your faith

Create a list of exciting web sites and share them with others and visit them yourself

Visit my website!

Write a list of 100 ways God has blessed you and your life

Visit the local library

Take deep breaths and stretch

Get back to work! Or start a project for work early

Put on a Christian CD and start worshipping

Do something crafty or artistic just for fun (even if you throw it out afterwards)

Visit a second hand shop and look for a good bargain

Play solitaire

Make that long overdue dentist/doctor appointment

Try on the clothes in your wardrobe

Clean the sock drawer

Learn a clean joke to tell others

Go fishing or just sit on the jetty and watch others do the work

Plan a camping trip

Lie on a hammock

Get into your hobbies

Adopt a baby for the day and give a tired mum a rest and a new challenge for yourself

Take some photos of 20 things that remind you of God's love

Write a poem

Walk through a nursery and view all the plants

Visit the pet shop and have a play with all the cute little animals

Clean your desk files out

Go out and collect shells or rocks

Help clean up your neighborhood by picking up some rubbish

Start a club and get others involved in your hobbies

Take a course offered by a Bible college or join a Bible study

Jump on a trampoline

Get a manual out and actually learn how to operate some of the gadgets around your house

Put new batteries in those watches or clocks or anything else that has stopped running in your household

Read the local newspaper to see what's on in your area

Find out when people's birthdays are and mark them on your calendar

Read a story into a recording device for someone who has difficulty reading or just for yourself to listen to in the car

Learn how to speak in another language

Learn how to say, 'I am cr you are beautiful' in as many languages as possible and say it a lot!

Stop and think about why you want to eat. Is there a problem that you need to solve, a relationship that you need to mend or end or something you need to examine more closely about who you are and why you act the way you do? Take a few moments and really think through your actions.

Brush your teeth

Make a gift for a friend

Go through all those photos and make a photo book
either online or the paper version
Pretend you are on vacation in your own town and see
some of the places you haven't been to in awhile
(take a friend with you for even more fun)
Take a Bite of Life Course

My Experience of the Bite of Life Course

Tracy Harrison

The Bite of Life course is something I can passionately recommend. As a result, I am excitedly anticipating the release of this book. I have done the course three times and each time God has brought me further along in my journey to healing. I have already experienced healing in the spiritual and the emotional sense. I am just beginning to see the physical side of that healing.

The first time I did the course was one of the hardest times in my relationship with God. My Grandmother who had raised me had just passed away and God had just begun the process of preparing my husband and I for long-term mission work. I was frustrated with the unknown and hurting with the loss.

When Marla rang and asked me to run the crèche for her course, it was a welcome relief of distraction. But each week the kids fell asleep or didn't come and as I sat in on the course, I heard the Lord speaking through his vessel. The Biblical truths week after week, reminded me that God had created me and wanted to guide me and comfort me through this time. But he also revealed to me that I was fearful of other adults and as a result of poor self-esteem had no boundaries with adults. My journey had begun. I was not healed but I was on my way.

A short time later, I approached a friend who was struggling in her walk with the Lord. I thought that she would benefit from the course and I took her along. But I soon learned the course was just as much for me to continue with. I learned during this period that God wanted me to have healthy boundaries and that the Bible speaks of the boundaries God has set in place for us. On judgment day when He asks me how I have treated His living temple, He is not going to want to hear, "Well God, ahhh …I've decided to do extensions!"

As I begun to understand the spiritual boundaries, they began to flow into the physical. I felt God healing the pain of abandonment I had as a child. He helped me to see how special I was to him. The God of the universe had created me and valued me and desired me to grow up spiritually. By the end of this course I was able to look into the mirror with God. I stood there before him a lot smaller then my actually size but with less shame and fear of rejection.

Then finally, I came again a third time; this time "for my husband's sake". This was the first of the couple's courses; But again it was really God continuing me along the journey. God was raising me up, not to give me self-confidence but a God-confidence to set boundaries in my life and go deeper into my relationship with him. The fear of rejection was gone and I felt a new boldness. I now can look into the mirror with God and see myself as I am.

God loves me the way I am. I may not be exactly the way he created me to be but I have dealt with the spiritual issues that were barriers and obstacles to my weight. Now, by Gods grace I am beginning the physical journey to restoring Gods temple not through the methods taught by systems of this world but methods taught by God's word.

God has revealed to me that thousands of women will be released from similar spiritual bondages. If this is you, grab a friend and a box of tissues and begin this journey together with God. It isn't easy but the freedom that you will receive as you mature in your relationship with God will be worth the effort.

For more information about
Bite of Life Courses that run
alongside the
'Hungry for Life' books
please visit the
'Hungry for Life' Facebook page or
email: **ozcamp@hotmail.com**

www.ingramcontent.com/pod-product-compliance
Lightning Source LLC
LaVergne TN
LVHW051550080426
835510LV00020B/2936